Social Cohesion
and Economic Prosperity

Social Cohesion
and Economic Prosperity

Jeff Dayton-Johnson

James Lorimer & Company Ltd., Publishers
Toronto, 2001

James Lorimer & Company Ltd. acknowledges the support of the Ontario Arts Council. We acknowledge the support of the Government of Canada through the Book Publishing Industry Development Program (BPIDP) for our publishing activities. We acknowledge the support of the Canada Council for the Arts for our publishing program.

Cover design: Shinn Design Inc.

National Library of Canada Cataloguing in Publication Data

Dayton-Johnson, Jeff
  Social cohesion and economic prosperity

Includes bibliographical references and index.
ISBN 1-55028-737-0 (bound)   ISBN 1-55028-715-X (pbk.)

1. Economics – Sociological aspects. 2. Social participation.
3. Social participation – Canada. 4. Canada – Economic conditions
– 1991-   . 5. Canada – Social conditions – 1991-   . I. Title.

HM548.D39 2001   306.3   C00-933239-1

James Lorimer & Company Ltd., Publishers
35 Britain Street
Toronto, Ontario
M5A 1R7

Printed and bound in Canada

Contents

Acknowledgements

Most of what follows is the result of several on-going and unfinished conversations with friends, colleagues and students. Most of them will recognize their ideas in the chapters ahead. A few read the manuscript with great care and merit special thanks: Lars Osberg (Dalhousie University), David Robinson (Laurentian University) and my student Frédéric Beauregard-Tellier. I only hope they will forgive me for not incorporating their suggestions more assiduously than I did. The book is better for their contributions.

The book is dedicated to Jennifer, Allie, and Nell; they already know why.

Halifax, Nova Scotia
January 2001

1

Introduction

In January 2000, Canada's Industry Minister, John Manley, proposed government subsidies to Canadian teams in the National Hockey League; team owners (notably those in the Ottawa Valley) had complained that differences in the tax treatment of US and Canadian teams put the latter at a significant financial disadvantage. This disadvantage, in turn, might eventually lead Canadian teams to follow the Québec Nordiques and Winnipeg Jets south of the border. Manley's move met with unanimous disapproval: how could the government judge this a better use for scarce resources in the face of homelessness, continued stubborn unemployment, various calls for middle-class tax relief, and generalized anxiety about the state of the health care system? Under the barrage of opposition, the proposal was speedily withdrawn.

In fact, disapproval of Manley's suggestion was not entirely unanimous. Rick Salutin, playwright, gadfly, and *Globe and Mail* columnist, justified the proposal after the fact. Hockey, for Salutin, is part of the glue that cements Canadian society. If Canada were to lose its NHL franchises, this would constitute a genuine fraying of the social fabric that binds Canadians together. Salutin even went so far as to cite Karl Polanyi, expatriate Austrian journalist and erstwhile economic historian, who, according to Salutin, "said that in harsh times — *especially* in severe crises — what keeps people going is not the stuff of sheer survival but the cultural sense that tells them who they are and that their lives make sense in the setting of neighbours and community." Huddling around Canadian Broadcasting Corporation broadcasts of *Hockey Night in Canada* provides to viewers just such an affirmation of identity and connectedness.

Stranger still than the newfound enthusiasm of the left-leaning Salutin for subsidies to multi-million-dollar corporations, perhaps, is the spectre of the World Bank seeking to build something called social capital. The multilateral lending institution increasingly seeks to promote projects that will increase or exploit the density of social networks and the interconnectedness of a nation's citizens — exactly the positive by-products of *Hockey Night in Canada* praised by Rick Salutin. What sets the Bank's view apart from Salutin's is a belief that such social capital will enhance economic performance. If we take them at their word, the Bank is suggesting that if more Angolans joined local football teams, they would improve the economic lot of Angola as a whole. So big dams and fiscal discipline are out, and soccer is in?

Scratch just little beneath the surface, and his idea does not seem so peculiar. If people tend to join voluntary organizations, they know more people, share more information, and perhaps even trust each other more. It's not surprising that the economy would run a little more smoothly. Likewise, if people feel they are part of a larger collective — all gathered round the CBC for *Hockey Night in Canada* — they might also be more prone to trust each other and the economy might reflect that trust in better performance. Not so strange, but not obvious either. And certainly not the orthodox view, not yet.

Knitted Warmth, around the World and across Canada

Globalization, the creation of truly worldwide markets, has left in its train both tremendous prosperity and painful dislocations. As markets for many goods and services become planetary in scope, families, neighbourhoods, and communities are subjected to new forces and pressures. Fleet-footed international investors might uproot a factory from its location of fifty years, only to re-establish it elsewhere, where costs are lower. The Québec Nordiques might reappear as the Colorado Avalanche. Young people seek jobs hundreds of kilometres from their childhood homes, perhaps even in other countries. Erratic work schedules and insecurity regarding long-term employment make it difficult for workers to volunteer after hours, or to join bowling leagues. In the globalizing world, there is increasing concern for the fate of social cohesion, the networks of social relationships that bind people together in communities, neighbourhoods, states and provinces, and countries. Each of the examples cited above — Rick Salutin's defence of government subsidies for Canadian hockey teams and the World Bank's enthusiasm for soccer clubs and farmers' organizations — would have sounded remarkably far-fetched even ten years ago, but both are leading indicators of a groundswell of attention to something called variously *social capital* or *social cohesion.*

Perhaps the vision of social cohesion that most readily comes to mind is that of the idealized, tight-knit rural community or urban neighbourhood. A resident of such a community who falls on hard times is propped up by his neighbours. Extended families and neighbours jointly look after children, providing a rich and warm environment in which to grow. The collective mobilizes to provide local needs like volunteer fire departments and amenities like parks. An equally important, and probably more relevant, model of social cohesion in the age of mass society is a nation-state composed largely of total strangers knit together by fellow feeling. An individual might not know the man seated next to her on the bus in the morning, but she shares this public space with him, and is reasonably confident that he too watched *Hockey Night in Canada* last night. People in this society are relatively less likely to commit crimes and relatively more likely to pay their taxes than in a country with less social cohesion.

That joining voluntary organizations is a good thing, that dense social networks enrich the lives of people and communities — these ideas date back to the dawn of liberal democracies and further. The idea that the social fabric is fraying is not altogether new either. Indeed, in Ernest Buckler's classic novel *The Mountain and the Valley* (1952), set in Nova Scotia's Annapolis Valley, protagonist David Canaan considers his village and muses that, over time, "the knitted warmth between its people had ravelled, until each was almost as alone in his own distraction now as the city people were ..." Canaan notes two things: a difference between the level of knitted warmth between country and city people, and a general decline in the overall level of knitted warmth, both *ostinato* themes in Canadian letters. Do people in some places enjoy more social cohesion than people elsewhere? And is the level of social cohesion (un)ravelling?

There are surprisingly large international differences in measures of this knitted warmth. Consider trust, a commonly consulted measure of social cohesion. If people feel a kinship with others, whether it is social or cultural or economic, they are arguably more likely to trust other people. Much of the remainder of this book will be given over to an exploration of the economic consequences of that trust. For the moment, it is interesting to note that there are broad international differences in the degree to which people claim to trust each other. The World Values Survey asked more than 80,000 people in nearly 50 countries whether they agreed with the statement that "in general, most people can be trusted." Table 1.1 shows the percentage of those asked, in selected countries, who agreed with the statement. The percentage ranges from about seven percent in Brazil and ten percent in Turkey, to 60 percent in Norway, Sweden, China, and Finland. (The countries are ranked from highest to lowest level of trust.) About half of Canadians report that people can be trusted; the proportion is more or less the same in the United States.

Table 1.1: Trust around the World

Norway	60.69	Belgium	30.63
China	59.63	Mexico	30.24
Sweden	59.60	Bulgaria	28.72
Finland	59.52	Austria	28.36
Denmark	55.53	Czechoslovakia	27.79
The Netherlands	53.39	Estonia	27.58
Canada	50.65	South Africa	26.63
USA	48.46	Switzerland	26.53
Eire	46.80	Belarus	25.02
Northern Ireland	42.76	Hungary	23.82
Great Britain	42.14	East Germany	22.38
Iceland	41.74	Argentina	22.36
Japan	37.59	Chile	22.07
Russia	35.61	Nigeria	21.40
Italy	35.11	France	21.36
South Korea	33.57	Portugal	20.72
Spain	31.63	Latvia	19.05
Poland	31.34	Slovenia	16.33
India	31.15	Romania	15.78
West Germany	31.08	Turkey	9.81
Lithuania	30.80	Brazil	6.60

Percentage of people who agree that "in general, people can be trusted."
Source: WVS (1999).

Within countries, too, there are regional differences in the level of reported trust. Based on the same survey, Table 1.2 shows the level of trust in ten Canadian provinces. Just over a third of New Brunswickers agree that most people can be trusted, a level similar to Italy, Spain, South Korea, and Russia. Newfoundlanders and Québecers are in the same range. Nearly two thirds of Albertans and British Columbians, however, trust others, similar to the highest-trust countries in the world (in Northern Europe and Scandinavia). (The highest average level of trust in Canada comes from Prince Edward Island, but we cannot be too confident about this result, as it is based on a very small number of surveys.) This survey evidence demonstrates a steady rise in people's trust as one moves from east to west in Canada.

Table 1.2: Trust across Canada

British Columbia	64.85
Alberta	65.51
Saskatchewan	52.75
Manitoba	55.76
Ontario	52.90
Québec	35.46
New Brunswick	34.27
Nova Scotia	52.06
Prince Edward Island	83.50
Newfoundland	38.99

Percentage of people who agree that "in general, most people can be trusted." Source: WVS (1999).

Another indicator of the level of social cohesion might be people's propensity to join voluntary organizations like political parties and choral groups. In some societies, people are more likely to join such groups than are people in other societies. The World Values Survey mentioned above also asked people about the types of organizations they belong to, and for whom they do volunteer work. The types of groups that the survey asked people about included the following categories: social welfare; religious/church organizations; education/ cultural groups; trade unions; political parties; community action; third world development; environment; professional associations; youth work; sports/recreation; women's groups; peace movement; animal rights; health-voluntary. Table 1.3 shows, for several countries, the percentage of people who are members of at least *one* of these groups, as well as the percentage of people who do unpaid or volunteer work for at least one of these groups. (Here the countries are ranked by the rate of membership, the numbers in the second column.)

Table 1.4, finally, shows the rate at which Canadians in each province join groups and do volunteer work. Like Table 1.3, this table reports the percentage of people in each province who are members of at least one group, and the percentage of people who perform unpaid work for at least one group.

Table 1.3: Associational Life, Selected Countries

Country	Member of one or more groups	Volunteer for one or more groups
Iceland	89.89	35.90
Sweden	85.00	39.16
East Germany	84.06	40.12
The Netherlands	82.72	35.34
Norway	81.19	36.56
Denmark	80.87	25.73
Finland	76.53	44.73
Estonia	73.21	33.53
Russia	71.69	21.56
South Korea	71.22	19.82
USA	70.55	45.47
Latvia	68.33	36.10
West Germany	66.74	30.55
Canada	63.57	42.81
Lithuania	60.10	30.20
China	58.11	60.10
Belgium	58.04	28.02
Northern Ireland	55.92	25.66
Great Britain	53.12	16.22
Austria	52.95	25.75
Hungary	50.15	16.42
Eire	48.70	26.50
Chile	45.00	29.60
Brazil	41.79	25.55
Bulgaria	40.72	19.73
Italy	39.06	26.58
Slovenia	38.55	15.17
France	37.52	23.25
Portugal	35.88	19.20
Mexico	35.79	25.87
Romania	30.37	25.02
Japan	30.17	13.65
Argentina	24.25	15.67
Spain	23.39	6.7

Percentage of people who are members of at least one type of group (second column), or who volunteer for at least one type of group (third column). Source: WVS (1999).

Table 1.4: Associational Life, Canada

Province	Membership in at least one group	Volunteer for at least one group
Prince Edward Island	82.08	82.08
Manitoba	77.58	57.41
Saskatchewan	67.01	49.53
Ontario	66.53	40.72
British Columbia	64.82	42.58
Québec	61.55	40.70
New Brunswick	51.92	42.24
Newfoundland	48.58	43.61
Nova Scotia	44.54	38.81

Percentage of people who are members of at least one type of group (second column), or who volunteer for at least one type of group (third column). Source: WVS (1999).

Rates of voluntary activity are more similar from province to province than are rates of trust, and rates of membership in groups show even less variation across the provinces than voluntary activity. Membership and voluntarism do not march in lock step with trust — in Table 1.4, the Prairies lead the country in associational life, rather than the higher-trust West. Atlantic Canada remains in last rank. No Canadian province exhibits the high rates of associational activity of Northern European countries (if we ignore, again, the Prince Edward Island figure, which is suspect because of the small sample size on which it is based).

What the survey evidence in Tables 1.1 through 1.4 demonstrates are the incredible international differences in measures of trust and associational life, both of which are likely to be reflections of social cohesion: these variations are mirrored within Canada as well. While it is impossible to say, based on this evidence, whether trust in others or the voluntary spirit is on the decline in those countries, one cannot help but note wide variations from country to country. Clearly, under different sets of conditions, like the level of economic development, different levels of social cohesion will emerge. In the face of this evidence, social scientists, including sociologists, psychologists, anthropologists, and political scientists, have ample reason to study the factors that determine a society's level of social cohesion.

An Economic Payoff?

This book will answer a different question: to what extent do these differences in social cohesion lead to differences in economic performance? Concern with what Buckler called a society's "knitted warmth" is evidently an old one. What is perhaps more novel is the notion, embodied in the World Bank's enthusiasm for soccer clubs and farmers' groups, that this knitted warmth might have an economic payoff. Can social cohesion make economies run more smoothly? Do societies where people are more prone to join groups and volunteer, and where people (perhaps not at all coincidentally) trust one another more, have faster rates of economic growth? The answer to both questions appears to be yes. Nations where people report higher levels of trust in others have faster-growing economies and higher rates of investment in new capital equipment. In poor agrarian countries, communities where people have a greater tendency to join voluntary organizations also tend to be home to people with higher incomes. (The evidence is reviewed and analyzed in detail in Chapters 2 and 3.)

Current concerns in Canada and elsewhere stem from a worry that the vigorous market forces unleashed by globalization will erode the social fabric; nevertheless, those people who worry about social cohesion generally acknowledge that globalization will improve economic performance. In this view, there is a trade-off between economic prosperity and preserving the existing network of social ties in our society. What this book will suggest is that this picture is too simplistic. In fact, market economies rely on a certain level of social cohesion to function effectively, and to the extent that current changes in policies tend to diminish social cohesion, they will weaken the effectiveness of the market economy to deliver livelihoods and innovation. Those who believe in a trade-off between economic performance and social cohesion will be disappointed by the negative economic consequences of weakened social cohesion. This book will show why this is so.

A Brief Intellectual History of Social Cohesion

The following chapters will define social cohesion more precisely: for the moment, let's take it to signify Buckler's "knitted warmth," the interconnectedness and trust among a group of people. The link between social cohesion and economic performance, for policy-makers, concerned citizens, and researchers, is intimately tied up with the aforementioned concept of *social capital*. Social cohesion may be a good thing in itself — this is the content of Salutin's defence of the NHL bailout. But the term social capital immediately invokes the economic realm, where "capital" is a well-understood concept. Or is it?

Economists have a disturbing proclivity for taking commonly used English words and employing them in ways that differ significantly from their commonly understood meaning. Examples include *rent, profit, cost, investment,* and *capital*. Capital, as the word is employed in classical economics, refers to current sacrifices that improve future economic well-being. A society can consume all of its current production today, or it can set aside some of that production — in the form of machines and factories and the like — to further increase production, and hence consumption, in the future. In the last half century, economists have argued that this *physical* capital, machine tools and railroad cars, is not the only kind of capital. We also invest in *human* capital when we sacrifice labour-market earnings today in order to get an education that leads to even higher labour-market earnings in the future. Even more recently, many have argued that this capital metaphor can be extended to our understanding of environmental resources, like a fish stock or the biosphere.

Social capital, then, refers to something about the interconnectedness of people that (a) requires some sacrifice of resources in the present, and (b) improves economic outcomes for those same people some time in the future. Social networks clearly require investments of time, money, and effort on the part of the people who constitute them (even if the "investors" are not always conscious of these costs). But do they enhance economic performance? If so, how? (A further source of confusion regarding common usage emerges for French speakers, for whom *capital social* refers to the sum of the initial contractual contributions made by the shareholders who comprise a corporation, something altogether different.)

Researchers typically credit US economist Glenn Loury with coining the term social capital in a 1977 article; more assiduous students have traced the term back to a US social reformer in 1920 (Feldman and Assaf, 1999). Indeed, the idea, if not the term, is frequently attributed to Alexis de Tocqueville, the French diplomat and political scientist whose *Democracy in America* (1835/1840) recounts his impressions of social organization in the then-very-young United States. De Tocqueville was struck by the dynamic material prosperity of the young country, but also by its rich associational life: "Americans of all ages, all conditions, and all dispositions, constantly form associations ... religious, moral, serious, futile, general or restricted, enormous or diminutive ... to give entertainments, to found seminaries, to build inns, to construct churches, to diffuse books, to send missionaries to the antipodes ..." (p. 198). De Tocqueville found this associational propensity to be inextricably linked to the democratic impulse, as opposed to the Old World political models. Indeed, as he wrote, "Wherever, at the head of some new undertaking, you see the government in France, or a man of rank in England, in the United States you will be sure to find an association" (ibid.).

The notion that civil society, the vast web of voluntary organizations, might be a substitute for the state (and for aristocracy) is the source of much of social capital's appeal in an ideological climate increasingly hostile to government intervention in the economy. Nevertheless, much of the recent research suggests that social capital is not so much a substitute for the state as it is a complementary factor that makes states do what they do better. Nowhere is this better clarified, perhaps, than in the groundbreaking research of US political scientist Robert Putnam.

Putnam, like de Tocqueville, explains the performance of democratic institutions in terms of the vibrancy of civic networks. Putnam's 1993 book *Making Democracy Work* looks at a unique political experiment in Italy. In the early 1970s, regional governments there were given vastly enhanced powers previously held by the central government. The form of the local governments was more or less identical in each case, but as the decades wore on, some regions (like Emilia-Romagna in the north) enjoyed responsive and efficient local governments, while others (like Basilicata in the south) suffered inefficient government performance and surly public servants. Putnam measures government performance by indicators such as the provision of daycare centres and family clinics, and bureaucratic responsiveness to citizens' inquiries. Local Italian governments that score better in these areas, Putnam claimed, do so because they serve a public with high levels of civic engagement. Where people are engaged — reading newspapers, interacting with others in dense social networks, voting in elections — governments are better at providing services. It is not difficult to imagine why this is so: an engaged public monitors its public servants and demands better accountability and responsiveness from them.

That an engaged constituency enjoys better government performance than a less-engaged one, *even when the formal apparatus of government is identical*, has obvious political consequences. It is not too much of a stretch to see that this has economic consequences as well. Governments and states in every country provide a range of economically-productive goods and services. They build roads and maintain sewer systems and regulate business activity. If some governments provide these things more efficiently and responsively, that will benefit the economy generally. Better-built and maintained roads reduce the cost of business for companies that transport goods and services. Better-maintained sewer systems enhance the quality of life for people and, all other things equal, will make people happier living and working in the area; with bad sewers, employers will have to pay more to prevent people from moving. Good government regulation clarifies the rules of economic behaviour and permits effective and low-cost enforcement of contracts and other agreements among parties. And so on. Following Putnam's work on Italy, then, we would expect that high levels of civic engagement should lead not only to better-performing governments, but also better-performing economies.

Putnam set out to answer the question, "Why do some regions in Italy have better-performing local governments?" In answering that question, he leaves us with another: "Where does high civic engagement come from?" He suggests that the answer to that question has to do with different levels of social cohesion in different regions of Italy. Putnam defines social capital as based on "social trust," trust not in a handful of family members and close friends, but instead trust in others generally. Social trust, in turn, is based on norms of reciprocity and interpersonal networks. Norms are informal rules of conduct to which all members of a community adhere to greater or lesser degree (like not littering); certain co-operative norms, based on the notion of reciprocity among people, facilitate higher levels of trust. Civic networks, built up when people belong to sports clubs or choral societies or political parties, increase the frequency with which people interact; when organizations are successful, they demonstrate to their members the possibilities and benefits of collective undertakings. To finish (for now) with Italy: why is there more social capital or social cohesion in some regions than in others? Because, centuries ago, historical evolution favoured more successful norms of reciprocity and civic networks in some regions. A very learned conclusion, but not one that is especially encouraging for policymakers and citizens concerned with improving the lot of regions with low levels of social cohesion.

Thus, the wellspring of the benefits of civic engagement in Italy discovered by Putnam derives, ultimately, from trust among people. International and interprovincial differences in trust exhibited in Tables 1 and 2 above, therefore, are critical to the civic life of those regions. Trust, indeed, is emphasized by another political scientist, Francis Fukuyama, in a pair of weighty tomes, *Trust: The Social Virtues and the Creation of Prosperity* (1995) and *The Great Disruption: Human Nature and the Reconstitution of Social Order* (1999). (Fukuyama, once an analyst for the US Department of State, earlier wrote a celebrated essay on "The End of History," interpreted by many as jingoistic triumphalism regarding the end of the Cold War; it concluded that liberal capitalist states were the only option for countries now, a view shared by Baroness Thatcher. As such, he became a darling of conservative intellectuals, and his aggressive entry into studies of social cohesion marked the appropriation of much of the social-capital discourse by the right in the US.)

Fukuyama's ambitious books underscore several of the points made by Putnam. "[T]rust arises when a community shares a set of moral values in such a way as to create expectations of regular and honest behavior" (p. 153). Such generalized trust makes possible many types of economic activity that would be difficult in its absence: notably, co-operation among people in large organizations like government agencies and corporations. In his 1999 book, *The Great Disruption ...*, Fukuyama even more ambitiously takes on the general theme of the construction of social capital. He traces the "great disruption" — marked by the usual indicators of social decay, such as out-of-wedlock births and crime rates, compellingly documented — to the onset of the information age. Nevertheless, a process of "renorming" is occurring as inherently social and rational people seek to spontaneously rebuild social capital appropriate to the new era.

Putnam and Fukuyama underscore the importance of "expectations of regular and honest behavior" to prosperity and democracy; this is a fundamentally economic argument linking social cohesion and economic growth. A complementary but non-economic mechanism has of late emerged as well. In this view, the globalization of markets will indeed bring about remarkable economic advances, but at the same time, globalization might fray the social fabric. The fear then is that insecurity and dislocation, even in the context of generally rising prosperity, will lead people to mobilize against the manifestations of globalization, thereby quashing the prosperity it brings.

This might be called the "backlash hypothesis," and its true intellectual forebear was none other than Karl Polanyi, the Austrian writer cited by Rick Salutin in his defence of Ottawa Senators owner Rod Bryden. (Polanyi, in fact, is enjoying a vogue in the last fifteen years or so that likely outshines his prominence while alive.) Polanyi sketched the historical emergence of the market economy in the eighteenth century, followed by a nineteenth-century backlash or countermovement: a "deep-seated movement sprang into being to resist the pernicious effects of a market-controlled economy. Society protected itself against the perils inherent in a self-regulating market system ..." (1944, p. 76).

Protestors against the World Trade Organization meetings in Seattle in 1999 and the World Bank–International Monetary Fund meetings in Washington, DC in 2000 clearly agreed with a fraction of the Backlash Hypothesis — that globalization weakens communities and social organization — and just as clearly confirm another part of it — that people will mobilize — by their actions. Who believes in *all* of the Backlash Hypothesis? None other than the Canadian government, it turns out, as well as several important members of the European Union, all of whom to greater or lesser degree advocate policies to counteract the ravelling nature of globalization of markets. These governments have bought into the beneficial effects of a liberal economy, but worry that a completely liberal economy contains the seeds of its own destruction. In this view, social cohesion is important to the functioning of the economy in a very political sense: without policies to safeguard social cohesion (which will, by the way, be explored in some detail in Chapter 7 of this book), citizens will push for policies that harm economic growth. That is, citizens distressed by the erosion of publicly-provided services will demand measures (publicly funded health care, welfare, unemployment insurance, and other costly means of promoting social stability) that impede the growth of unfettered capitalism — thus "shooting themselves in the foot" by impairing their own potential prosperity.

The amount of research on social capital and social cohesion is large, interdisciplinary, and growing; this chapter does not claim to be exhaustive in its coverage. This summary of some of the more celebrated research reveals two channels through which social cohesion affects the economy. The first, emphasized especially by Fukuyama and others who concentrate on the functional role of trust, is microeconomic. Social cohesion enhances the prospects for the mutually-beneficial exchanges that underlie the success of the market economy. This book will emphasize this channel, in part because its logic is fundamentally economic, in keeping with the aim and tenor of this book. The second channel, stressed by Putnam, is political: cohesive societies monitor their governments better, which is good for the economy in turn. This is also the channel at work according to the Backlash Hypothesis. As societies lose cohesiveness, their members mobilize to circumscribe the market forces that ravel their cohesiveness, and incidentally, deliver prosperity.

Also, although this quick and general review of the intellectual history of social cohesion has failed to precisely define the term (except to use Ernest Buckler's definition), we would do well to focus on three dimensions of the phenomenon. These are the three empirical manifestations of social cohesion that Putnam focuses on: trust, norms, and networks. Chapter 3 will attempt to weave these elements into a unified theory of sorts.

My Personal History with Social Cohesion: Tales from Rural Mexico

All of this illustrates why an intellectually curious economist or observer of social affairs might have come across the issue of social cohesion in recent years. But it does not tell you how I came to devote so much of my time to issues of social cohesion and economic prosperity. That story begins in the mid-1990s on the arid high plains of Central Mexico. There, in the rural regions of the state of Guanajuato, I was a graduate student carrying out field research on local management of small-scale irrigation systems known in Mexico as *unidades de riego*. These systems, typically based on a crude technology, are collectively owned by small groups of farmers, who are in turn collectively responsible for their maintenance, and for the distribution of irrigation water. I wanted to know what leads some communities to use these collective assets judiciously while other groups fail to translate such resources into higher crop yields. Why do some people co-operate while others do not?

I visited over fifty farming communities with collectively-managed irrigation systems: reservoirs of some kind and a canal network. Some observations from just two extreme cases, however, illustrate the range of success and failure of various communities. Consider the small *unidad* Nuestra Señora del Rosario in the impoverished Ocampo region of the state. (All names of people and *unidades* in this little history are fictitious.) There are five irrigating farm households at Rosario, who formed a water users' association in 1983. The farmers have not irrigated for several years, but the problem has not been one of water scarcity. The farmer on whose land the levee sits (Don Leonardo) will not release water for irrigation, and any semblance of a water users' association has disappeared. The week before I surveyed the farmers at Rosario, the four farmers other than Don Leonardo sought me out at my hotel, with a litany of complaints against Don Leonardo: not only had he refused to let anyone near the water, he allegedly stole some of their sheep, too. Later, as I inspected the state of repair of the canals at Rosario, Don Leonardo appeared and dominated the discussion. He subscribes to the legal interpretation that he who owns the land on which the levee is located owns the levee, which is not true under Mexican water law. He made reference to periods in the past when he could not be present to participate in water-use affairs because (i) he was driving a bus and (ii) he was in prison.

During the tense discussion, Don Porfirio, leader of the other faction, craftily sought to take advantage of the presence of my survey team to propose the formation of a brand-new leadership council, and cagily he asked Don Leonardo who he would like to see as president. Now even Leonardo could not nominate himself, so he reluctantly agreed with the others that Porfirio should be president. But then he rallied: he proposed that one of his sons should be secretary. Given that Leonardo farms his sons' land, this was tantamount to nominating himself. More heated discussion followed but there was no resolution. I am not optimistic that those incipient attempts to re-establish common-property resource management at Rosario ever bore fruit.

The poorer community of San Sergio, a couple of hours' bumpy ride from Rosario, provides a telling contrast. San Sergio comprises 84 households; the water users' association dates from the land reform era of 1936. Each farm household has three irrigated plots, each in one of three irrigation zones, to compensate for irregularities in the distribution of water. A small modern dam irrigates one zone; two colonial-era (i.e., eighteenth-century) dams irrigate the other two. The farmers at San Sergio managed six or seven episodes of irrigation-water distribution per year, in contrast to one or two in neighbouring communities. The greater frequency of application of irrigation water makes possible the cultivation of slightly higher-valued crops, like the *mulato* chile, which require more careful water management. Some of the marketing of chiles is collectively organized, garnering better prices for the farmers than would obtain if all sold individually to local middlemen.

What accounts for the marked differences between Rosario and San Sergio? The conventional wisdom among irrigation specialists is that poorly-performing irrigation systems need infusions of physical capital: repair to levees and canals, installation of modern water-control structures to replace primitive earthen gates. Indeed, at the time I was in the field in Mexico, the national water commission was negotiating this type of physical improvement program, with hopes that it would be financed by the World Bank, among other sources. I wrote a summary of my research findings for the state office of the national water commission in which I stressed that, while physical capital might not hurt, these communities were most in need of *social* capital. Where there was a history of collective action and working together, communities did a better job solving problems associated with irrigation (and indeed, with the precarious nature of agricultural livelihoods more generally). My research also provided a few initial clues about why some communities succeed and others fail to construct social capital. I was particularly struck by the finding that average wealth levels were not the sole determinant of success. Both Rosario and San Sergio are located in the poorest agricultural zone of my study area. Notably, a relatively equitable distribution of land-holding was associated with better maintenance and with better-performing local rules. San Sergio has perfect equality of land-holding, and scattering of individual household plots to equalize exposure to risk; Rosario has among the highest levels of inequality among the communities I visited.

My sojourn in rural Mexico convinced me that economic prosperity is as closely linked to the quality of social relationships as is to investment in physical capital. (One consequence is that we will return to farmers and canals at several points in the remainder of this book.) How could these lessons, I wondered, be transferred to the setting of the relatively prosperous, urbanized economy of Canada? This book attempts to answer that question.

An Outline of the Book

This book is fundamentally inspired by the conviction that economic analysis is a constructive way of understanding social problems. An economic analysis of "knitted warmth" may be in its infancy, but I argue that it will be productive. This book does not presuppose a detailed familiarity on the part of the reader with the usual tools of economic analysis, which include complicated mathematical and statistical elements. Indeed, one of the objectives of this book, perhaps the chief one, is to synthesize and diffuse the specialized research on this topic for a wider audience. Nevertheless, the book does presume an interest in economic affairs and, for those hostile to economists and their way of thinking, a willing suspension of disbelief. Along the way, I hope that the reader will learn something not only about the economic analysis of social cohesion, but also about other economic topics and, more broadly, about the way that economists make their points. In particular, the book is directed at university students of sociology, public policy, and economics, at policy-makers, and especially at citizens-at-large with an interest in the functioning of the economic system in which we are all enmeshed.

At the same time, I hope that the discussion will be of interest to professional social scientists in academia, government, and elsewhere. Economists in particular will recognize that this is what Keynes called an "essay in persuasion," and not the usual product of scholarly labour that characterizes our fraternity/sorority. Such readers will be especially aware of the extent to which the thoughts presented in this book are fundamentally borrowed from the many studies cited in the bibliography at the end of the book.

An explicit consideration of social cohesion and its effects may take economics where it has traditionally not chosen to tread, and may lead to conclusions that mainstream economics has not typically made. Nevertheless, this book will illustrate that these unorthodox questions are quite fruitfully analyzed using rather traditional methods of economic inquiry — more or less mathematical models based on rational choice and statistical analysis of economic data. This is not to say that a radical revisioning of economic method might not be a good idea; my aim is more modestly to demonstrate that there is a coolly rational case to be made for the economic virtues of communities and the interconnectedness of people.

The following two chapters sketch the macroeconomic and microeconomic dimensions of social cohesion. This introduction has shown that there are wide variations in trust and associational life among nations — markers of social cohesion. Chapter 2 will show that there are similarly remarkable variations in economic well-being among nations. This is not in itself particularly newsworthy, but Chapter 2 will also review evidence that suggests that the variation in social cohesion and the variation in economic well-being might be correlated; that is, trust might foment prosperity. Chapter 2 requires a tour of international statistical analysis. Chapter 3 introduces the microeconomic logic that might link social cohesion and better economic performance. There it is argued first that the modern market economy relies on a foundation of co-operative behaviour, and second, that social cohesion enhances the prospects for co-operative behaviour.

Chapter 4 provides illustrations of social cohesion in important parts of the economic fabric of society — in workplaces, in neighbourhoods, and in schools. There it will be shown that social cohesion can contribute not only to narrow measures of economic success (such as rates of growth of Gross Domestic Product), but especially to wider measures of well-being (like the United Nations Human Development Index).

Many authors and commentators have tended to regard social cohesion as synonymous with equality. I argue that the two terms are conceptually distinct, but that there is an important and close linkage between them. Highly unequal societies are unlikely to be cohesive, and egalitarian social policies are likely to promote social cohesion. Economic research in recent years has increasingly viewed economic inequality as harmful to economic growth. This research, and its link to social cohesion, is reviewed in Chapter 5.

Together with the recent upsurge in enthusiasm for social capital and social cohesion, there has been a recognition by many that these phenomena can have a downside. Groups with dense interconnectedness among their members and closely observed rules of conduct might be cohesive, but they might exploit their cohesiveness to predate upon the larger society. This is directly related to the theme of this book because such groups can have a negative impact on the performance of the economy. The Mafia is frequently posited as an example of this possibility: organized-crime groups seem to exhibit a high level of internal cohesion that, indeed, serves their economic aims, but at the same time harms the functioning of the larger economy and society in which they are situated. Moreover, fragmented societies often pit various cohesive groups against each other to disastrous effect, as between Protestants and Catholics in Ulster, or among the various regions of the former Yugoslavia. Chapter 6 discusses and interprets situations where social cohesion fails to deliver the (economic) goods.

When economists go on at length about some new model or theory — as I'm doing in this book — a fair question that is frequently thrown at them to try to contain their exuberance is, "So, what is the policy relevance?" How does an understanding of the economics of social cohesion change the way we think about economic policy-making? Many have argued that social cohesion is an important ingredient in the functioning of the economic system, but that it lies largely beyond the reach of policy-makers. In Chapter 7, I will argue that policy can in fact affect the level of social cohesion. In the first instance, it is clear that misguided policy can damage social cohesion. But I will also argue that policy can promote social cohesion, and that in a rich country like Canada, an understanding of social cohesion largely provides a renewed justification for many of the policies of the welfare state.

Although it is not the job of this book to issue a call for new ways to consciously engineer social cohesion in Canada, Chapter 8 does so nevertheless. The chapter argues that the costs of the most successful form of national-level social cohesion, nationalism, easily outweigh the benefits. I suggest we look to an idealized version of the modern city, rather than an idealized version of the small town, as an inclusive vision of the cohesive society.

Bibliographic Notes

Rather than litter the text with citations and footnotes, each chapter will include a brief bibliographic note with pointers to texts and sources not explicitly cited in the body of the chapter. Authors mentioned in each chapter can be found in the list of references at the end of the book.

Salutin (2000) includes the defence of the NHL subsidy scheme. Rosie DiManno (2000), perhaps less artfully, made the same case in the Toronto Star. On the intellectual history of social capital, Feldman and Assaf (1999) provide a useful annotated bibliography of the most noteworthy research. Knack (1999) makes the distinction between macro-political and microeconomic channels that link social cohesion and economic performance. The Backlash Hypothesis was formulated in a somewhat different manner by Polanyi (1944); the Canadian government's version of the story in the era of globalization can be found in a February 1999 report of the government-sponsored Policy Research Initiative (PRI, 1999) and in a June 1999 report of the Standing Senate Committee on Social Affairs, Science and Technology (SSCSAST, 1999). My Mexican irrigation study is described in greater detail in Dayton-Johnson (1999).

2

Knitted Warmth and the Wealth of Nations

In the late 1990s, the Canadian media paid substantial attention to an apparently abstruse debate among economists and government statisticians regarding manufacturing productivity in Canada and the US. Manufacturing productivity, briefly, is measured in this debate as the value of manufacturing output (in a year, say) per worker in the manufacturing sector. (Some divide manufacturing output by hours worked in manufacturing, others by employed worker in manufacturing.) Over time, indexes of manufacturing productivity have been rising in both North American economies, a sign of increased efficiency; that efficiency, in turn, reflects better educated and trained workers, investment in more machines and equipment, and the incorporation of new technologies and organizational innovations. During all of the last century, manufacturing productivity has been lower — on the order of 20 to 30 percent lower — in Canada relative to the US. Moreover, manufacturing productivity in the two countries has grown at more or less the same rate over the last century, so that there has been no narrowing of the gap.

The source of the controversy is the following: beginning in the 1980s, Canadian productivity growth in the manufacturing sector appeared to slow down relative to growth in US manufacturing. The consequence is that over time, the gap between manufacturing productivity in the two countries will expand. Some analysts, however, claim that problems with measuring output and differences in measurement between Canada and the US make it difficult to categorically claim that Canada's growth is lagging. Furthermore, even among those who believe that Canada's productivity is slowing, there are conflicting claims about the source of the divergence in the two countries' trends.

Perhaps what was most remarkable about this debate (which is far from settled) is the attention that was paid to it during the autumn of

1998 and the winter of 1999 in the national and local media in Canada. These are confusing quantitative arguments, based on levels of productivity, and also on rates of growth of productivity, a distinction lost on some newscasters and talk-radio hosts, who claimed that productivity had been "the same" in the two countries, but now Canada was "lower." In fact, Canadian productivity has always been lower, and even in sectors where Canadian productivity is growing faster than US productivity, the *level* of productivity continues to be lower. Despite these problems of interpretation, the Canadian public evinced a genuine curiosity regarding this debate over measurement and trends. Why? Probably because people recognize the close link between productivity and standards of living. Workers' earnings are tightly linked to productivity levels in the sector of the economy where they work; growth in earnings, similarly, is tied to growth in productivity. Indeed, it is not coincidental that the gap in average income between Canada and the US is more or less of the same size as the productivity gap between the countries.

The sources of rising living standards might not make for sensationalistic copy, but sometimes they make the news nevertheless. This is gratifying for economists given that, arguably, the most fundamental task of economics is to explain differences in prosperity. If the differences among countries in levels of social cohesion reported in the previous chapter appear large, they are dwarfed by differences in average income.

International Differences in the Standard of Living

Table 2.1 illustrates the average level of income in a small number of countries in 1998. The numbers reported here have been computed to facilitate comparison across countries. First, these incomes are measured in 1998 US dollars for all countries. Thus these comparisons are not complicated by distortions in exchange rates between countries. Second, these average incomes have been calculated using what economists call the *purchasing power parity* method: in essence, this means that 740 dollars of income in Mozambique will buy exactly as much as 740 dollars of income in France or the USA. This corrects for differences in prices for essentially similar things between rich and poor countries — a haircut is a haircut, and the purchasing power parity corrections mean that one hundred dollars buys just as many haircuts in France as it does in New Zealand.

Table 2.1: Per Capita Income

USA	29,240
Canada	22,814
France	21,214
New Zealand	16,084
Argentina	11,728
Latvia	5,777
Vietnam	1,689
Mozambique	740

Source: World Bank (2000).

The international differences reported in Table 2.1 might or might not be widely known, but they are genuinely staggering in their magnitude. They reveal that the average income in Canada is just over three-quarters of the average income in the US. Keep in mind just how large that difference looms in the Canadian media, and consider that the average income in Argentina is *one-half* of the Canadian average, or that the Latvian average is *one-fourth* the Canadian average. Indeed, the average person in countries like Canada, France, or New Zealand is more than ten times richer than the average person in Vietnam and close to *forty* times richer than the average person in Mozambique. Why are average incomes so vastly different among countries?

Standard models of economic growth identify two sources of economic growth: the accumulation over time of labour and of physical and human capital, and improvements in technology and the organization of production. Can economic growth theory, with its focus on the accumulation of productive factors, account for differences on the order of the gap between Canada and Mozambique? To date, its success has been mixed at best. Differences in savings behaviour (which determines the rate of physical-capital accumulation) and schooling (which determines the rate of human-capital accumulation) are incapable of explaining differences of the magnitude that separates Canada and Mozambique. Just as cosmologists cannot adequately account for the weight of the universe and thus resort to discussions of "dark matter," growth-accounting economists have resigned themselves to a large unexplained "residual."

It is in this context that unorthodox explanations for economic prosperity, like social cohesion, capture the imagination of researchers. Could differences in trust, social capital, social cohesion, and quality of community be part of the reason for these differences in per capita income levels? If we were to incorporate these variables into our statistical analysis of economic growth, would the size of the unexplained residual be reduced? We will return to this statistical detective story momentarily. First, we ask why social cohesion might matter for growth.

Trust and Trustworthiness

On 16 March 2000, the Halifax *Chronicle-Herald* reported that 23-year-old Jason Fitzgerald had found $1,000 worth of toonies in a bank parking lot at one in the morning, and returned them to the police. A surprised police spokesperson baldly stated that "[t]hat guy could've walked away with $1,000 but he didn't," a possibility that briefly crossed Fitzgerald's mind: "My first reaction was 'Wow, this could be my Visa bill.'" *Homo economicus*, the rational protagonist of economics textbooks, would have little trouble deciding what to do with a big bag of change found in the dark of night. But Fitzgerald turned the money over to police. His rationale was the following: "I work with kids and I try to instill good values in them ... It wouldn't be right if I were to turn around and do something like that." It is not too much of a stretch to claim that social cohesion, in part, changed the incentives facing Fitzgerald. As a co-ordinator for a youth centre, he is exercising civic engagement in precisely the way that Chapter 1 described the phenomenon. Chapter 3 will attempt to be more systematic in explaining why civic engagement and group member-ships makes co-operative behaviour more attractive to people, but the idea is intuitive enough.

So this Haligonian contributes to, and has been influenced by, social cohesion. The task of this book is to illustrate that such ges-tures are somehow good for the economy. How is Fitzgerald's ges-ture good for economic performance? By itself, it is not. But if this gesture is repeated by all or most people as a matter of course, it can have a profound economic impact. The bag of two-dollar coins in this incident was dropped in transit between two branches of the Royal Bank. As we all know, banks generally transport large quan-tities of specie only in heavily-guarded armoured cars. That is an expensive way to move things. If everyone could be counted on not to take what they do not own, and indeed to return others' lost items, however valuable, banks could transport money more cheaply and lower the cost of doing business. If the banking industry is suffi-ciently competitive, this translates into lower-cost service to custom-ers: lower fees, lower rates of interest on loans and mortgages, higher rates of interest on savings accounts. Many readers might mutter, well, good on the banks. Indeed, the thought experiment is a little forced: it is unlikely that banks (in Canada, at least) will ever transport large quantities of cash without (expensive) security measures; it is furthermore arguable that there is much competition in the Canadian banking industry.

But consider an even larger canvas. How much money is spent protecting property from being stolen or damaged by others? How much, in addition, is spent on building and running prisons, on the criminal-justice system as a whole? From a macroeconomic perspective, that sum represents resources that, in a higher-trust economy, could instead be devoted to research and development, to music programs in the schools, to daycare centres. At least some of those alternative expenditures would raise the rate of economic growth, relative to the current allocation of spending.

Or consider a small-scale example that arose during the writing of this book. I sought to consult the Francis Fukuyama book *Trust*, discussed in Chapter 1, while preparing the manuscript. The Dalhousie University Library lists *Trust* among its holdings, but the book is missing. It was either stolen or deliberately misplaced on another shelf. This is especially ironic, no? A library is a remarkable public resource, but one that relies on a fairly high level of trust in order to serve its users: *Trust* is missing from the Dal library because of a betrayal of that trust. This means that I had to use the Inter-library Loan service. The theft of the book imposed a cost of time and other resources on me and on the library staff. A higher-trust university community will have, all other things remaining the same, a lower-cost library system.

Look at it from the perspective of an individual entrepreneur. Suppose that this person has an idea that will create profits for her and employment for others. In a fragmented society with low levels of trust, it will be more difficult for her to secure start-up financing from a bank. Where trust is not a generalized phenomenon, where, in the words of Robert Putnam, "personal trust" has not become "social trust," would-be entrepreneurs' capacity to start new economic activities is frequently constrained by the lending possibilities of their immediate families — the only people who trust them. In a low-trust society, our potential entrepreneur might also face higher costs of doing business, perhaps because she has to spend more on security — after-hours guards, alarm systems, insurance costs. Costs might be higher for her because of the costs of writing elaborate contracts in place of handshake agreements with others. In sum, the same good idea might be an economically viable investment in a high-trust economy, but non-viable in a low-trust economy.

A completely trusting Eden like that depicted in this thought experiment might not exist, not now, not in history. But the hypothetical example suggests that differences in the level of trust, like the differences reported in Chapter 1 between different countries, could be reflected in different levels of economic performance. One final point to emphasize: trust of the type that favours economic performance is promoted by social cohesion. Our civically-engaged Haligonian opted against a theft with zero probability of detection precisely because he was civically engaged.

A problem in moving from our journalistic example to social science is that this is just one incident. We do not know how many $1,000 toonie bags are misplaced by the Royal Bank every year, and how many are not returned. There is insufficient evidence, thus, regarding the fraction of people in Canada who are trustworthy. Of course, the World Values Survey data, summarized in Tables 1.1 and 1.2, reveal the percentage of people in Canada and other countries who *trust* others, if not the fraction that are actually trust*worthy*. If we really want to know the fraction of trustworthy people, the fraction of trusting people might be a good substitute; after all, people come to trust others, over time, if they find them to be trustworthy.

It turns out that there is some slightly more systematic evidence about the degree to which people in various countries are trustworthy. *Readers Digest* magazine conducted an interesting experiment in 1996. Several wallets, containing considerable cash and identification of their fictitious owners, were strategically "lost" in a number of big cities in several countries; the number of wallets returned to their owners is an index of trustworthiness. World Bank economist Stephen Knack (2000) correlated the proportion of "lost" wallets returned in a country with the rate of trust in that country, from the World Values Survey. The correlation is quite good: countries where people are more likely to return lost wallets are also countries where people are more likely to trust other people. In Norway and Denmark, all wallets were returned, and the proportion of people who trust others is exceptionally high as well. In East Germany and Italy, between 20 and 30 percent of wallets were returned, and trust, accordingly, hovers around 20 to 30 percent. There are a few surprises. Sweden has the highest level of trust, over 60 percent, but Swedes returned lost wallets at the same rate as lower-trust countries like

Australia and Spain, where trust levels are only around 30 percent. France has low trust, but French people return wallets as frequently as the much higher trust Netherlands.

A number of studies have used the national-level trust data from the World Values Survey as a measure of a country's social cohesion in order to gauge the contribution of trust to economic growth. Moreover, the reader will recall that the World Values Survey also provides information regarding people's propensity to join organizations and perform volunteer work, further indicators of social cohesion. Growth studies using these and other measures of social cohesion are assessed in the remainder of this chapter.

Social Cohesion and the Macroeconomy: Evidence

Average income is not the only valid indicator of well-being, nor is growth of average incomes society's only goal. Nevertheless, economic growth — defined as sustained increase in the average income in a country — could do a great deal to improve the lot of people in Mozambique or Vietnam, on the evidence of Table 2.1. For this reason, economists continue to spend a lot of energy trying to determine the factors that lead to growth successes.

Table 2.2: Average Annual Growth, Selected Countries

Country	Growth, 1980–1990	Growth, 1990–1998
USA	1.3	1.8
Canada	1.1	0.8
France	1.4	1.0
New Zealand	-0.2	1.5
Argentina	-2.9	3.8
Latvia	3.9	-7.2
Vietnam	0.9	6.3
Mozambique	-3.5	3.1

Average annual rates of growth of per capita GDP, in percentage terms. Source: Computed from data in World Bank (1999), Tables 3 and 11.

Let us look again at the eight economies whose average income levels were reported in Table 2.1. Table 2.2 shows, for each of these economies, the average annual rate of growth of per capita GDP during the 1980s and during the 1990s (through 1998). Note that the usual economic growth statistics that are reported in the news refer to growth of GDP; the figures in Table 2.2 refer to growth of GDP per person. (This *per capita* growth rate is essentially equal to the rate of growth of GDP minus the rate of growth of population.) This distinction is especially important for countries like Vietnam and Mozambique in the table, which had relatively high rates of population growth during the 1980s. As with levels of average income, indeed, as with levels of trust and associational life, there is remarkable variation from country to country in economic growth rates. During the 1980s, the Mozambican average income contracted at a rate that averaged -3.5 percent per year, while Latvia's average income bounded ahead at nearly 4 percent per year. In the 1990s, the two economies' growth rate positions were reversed, as Latvia's average income suffered the transition to a market economy, shrinking more than 7 percent per year, while Mozambique enjoyed an enviable 3.1 percent growth.

What are the factors that explain these broad differences in economic growth, both across countries, and over time? Suppose that we had information on the growth rates during the 1980s and 1990s, as in Table 2.2, for a large sample of countries, as well as data on a number of characteristics of each of those countries. Generally speaking, an econometric analysis of the determinants of growth postulates a set of explanatory variables. The statistical test performs (at least) two functions: (i) it determines how much of the variation in international growth rates is explained by the set of variables chosen by the researcher; and (ii) it determines how much each single variable contributes to the explained variation.

Consider a classic in this genre, Harvard University economist and *Business Week* columnist, Robert J. Barro's 1991 article, "Economic Growth in a Cross Section of Countries." Like most such studies, the paper contains a multitude of statistical models, but one (his model (1) in the paper) will suffice to illustrate the kind of results that are generated. In the model, Barro is trying to explain the average annual rate of growth of per capita income between 1960 and 1985 for a group of 98 countries. The set of explanatory variables he uses to explain the international variation in growth rates includes, for each of those 98 countries:

- the *level* of per capita income in 1960
- the secondary school enrolment ratio in 1960 (defined as the share of secondary school-age children actually enrolled in school)

- the primary school enrolment ratio in 1960 (defined similarly to the secondary school ratio)
- government consumption spending (not including defence and education spending) as a fraction of GDP (averaged over the 25-year period)
- the number of revolutions and coups per year
- the number of assassinations per million people, each year
- a variable measuring the price of capital goods relative to their price in the US.

What does the exercise reveal? Table 2.3 presents the regression results more or less as they would appear in the actual article. One thing that the table does not show is how well this whole *set* of variables explains international variation in growth rates. For this sample of 98 countries, the chosen variables explain 56 percent of the observed variation in growth rates; this is the so-called "R-squared" statistic. Not bad, but it means that there are other variables out there that have an effect on growth rates.

Table 2.3: Explaining Economic Growth

Variable	Coefficient	t-statistic
Per capita income, 1960	-0.0075	-1.1
Secondary enrolment, 1960	0.0305	3.9
Primary enrolment, 1960	0.025	4.5
Government consumption	-0.119	-4.3
Revolutions	-0.0195	-3.1
Assassinations	-0.0333	-2.2
Investment costs	-0.0143	-2.7

Estimated coefficients (partial list), and t-statistics for a regression model explaining average real per capita GDP growth for the period 1960–1985, for a sample of 98 countries. Source: Barro (1991).

For each of the chosen explanatory variables, the table presents the estimated coefficient, a measure of the impact of that variable on growth rates. (The table also presents for each variable the t-statistic, a measure of how well the estimated coefficient is measured; it is based on the t-statistic that we make statements about "statistical significance.") Consider the effect of schooling; the enrolment ratios measured in 1960 give us an indication of the "human capital stock" at the beginning of the growth experience that the regression seeks to explain. The estimated coefficient on the secondary enrolment ratio is 0.0305 (and it is highly significant, for those who worry about such matters). What this means is that if a country were able, in 1960, to raise its secondary enrolment ratio by one percentage point, holding all other variables in the list unchanged, its subsequent average growth rate would be 0.305 percentage points higher over the next 25 years. If it had increased its secondary enrolment ratio by 21 percentage points (the standard deviation, or average deviation from the mean secondary enrolment ratio), a country would raise a growth rate of, say, 2.2 percent per year to 2.8 per cent per year. By 1985, the difference between 2.2 percent growth every year and 2.8 percent growth cumulates dramatically; with the higher growth rate, average income would be more than twenty percent greater than under the slower growth rate. Twenty percent higher income could make a big difference to the average income earner in Mozambique or Vietnam.

The results in Table 2.3 suggest that government consumption spending (which does not include investment in things like infrastructure or education), has a negative effect on growth. Not surprisingly, political instability as measured by coups and assassinations also has a negative effect.

Stepping back a bit, Barro's initial regression model tells us two things. It confirms the vital importance of education for economic growth. And second, it illustrates that close to half the story remains unexplained. Barro's study is not necessarily the best of its kind, although it was hugely influential. There have been many other such studies, using different time spans, different sets of variables, different sets of countries, different measures of economic performance.

Nevertheless, despite the number of new variables added into the regression equations (and some economists refer disparagingly to this research approach as "kitchen-sink regressions," suggesting that everything but the kitchen sink has been thrown in), the "residual" problem continues to bedevil researchers. And it is the unexplained residual that has led some of them to include measures of social cohesion in their regression equations. The results are surprising.

Evidence: Trust

Economists Stephen Knack and Philip Keefer included the World Values Survey trust variable in a series of Barro-style kitchen-sink growth regressions in a 1997 paper. Other variables mirrored those from Barro's study, listed in Table 2.3: included in the analysis were primary and secondary school enrolment ratios in 1960, average income in 1960, and the price level of investment goods (physical capital and the like) in 1980, relative to the United States. The authors confirmed that a country's rate of trust in 1980 was positively and significantly related to its growth rate in the period 1980–1992, and to the investment rate in the same period.

Knack and Keefer's results indicate that, all other things remaining the same, a ten-percentage-point increase in trust — the difference between France and West Germany, according to Table 1.1 — is associated with an increase in growth of four-fifths of a percentage point. France's per capita income growth rate over the period 1980–1992 was about 1.4 percent annually. A ten-percentage-point increase in the rate of trust would have raised that to about 2.2 percent. How much difference would this make? Consider a simple numerical illustration. If average income in 1980 was $10,000, average income in 1992 would be $11,816 with a growth rate of 1.4 percent, and $13,016 with a growth rate of 2.2 percent. The difference over the twelve-year span is nearly $1,200, or nearly 12 percent of the initial income level. Alternatively, with French levels of trust, West Germany's growth over the period would have averaged about 0.8 percent annually, rather than the actual average of 1.6 percent per year. If average income in West Germany had been $10,000 in 1980, it would have grown to $12,098 with a growth rate of 1.6 percent annually, and only $10,977 with a low-trust growth rate of 0.8 percent. All other things remaining equal, the benefit to West Germany of having a trust level ten percentage points higher than France would be equal to about $1,120 in average income over twelve years, or about 11 percent of the initial average income. This is a quantitatively big impact, comparable in magnitude to increasing the primary enrolment ratio by half a percentage point. Education has a larger impact, but the effect of trust is appreciable even on this scale.

A group of economists from Harvard University and the University of Chicago looked more closely at the effects of trust (using, again, the World Values Survey measure of trust) on variables other than economic growth and efficiency. Inspired by Fukuyama's views on trust (reviewed in Chapter 1), they looked at the effect of trust on fourteen outcomes. A country's level of trust, they found, has a significant impact on all of these outcomes, including positive effects on measures of government performance (efficiency of the judiciary, absence of corruption, bureaucratic efficiency, and tax compliance); participation in associations; and measures of "social efficiency" (quality and adequacy of infrastructure, lower levels of infant mortality, higher high school completion rates, lower levels of inflation).

One of Fukuyama's hypotheses is that generalized or social trust facilitates the formation of large organizations necessary for the efficient functioning of the modern economy, whether they are government bureaucracies or private corporations. In the absence of sufficiently high levels of social trust, smaller family-based firms will predominate. Accordingly, the Harvard-Chicago team calculated a measure of the sales of the twenty largest publicly-traded firms in a country as a percentage of that country's GDP: this is a measure of the prevalence of large firms in the economy. They find that trust has a positive and significant impact on the prevalence of larger corporations in a country, suggesting yet another channel through which trust affects the economy.

An interesting feature of the effect of trust is that it has a bigger impact on economic growth in poorer countries. Knack and Keefer found that the effect of a country's trust level on the average rate of economic growth in the 1980–1992 period is greater the *lower* the average income in that country in 1960. They interpret this as follows: Trust can serve as a substitute for an elaborate (and expensive) network of formal laws and contracts. If every transaction is backed up by an exhaustive contract that specifies what is to occur in every potential eventuality, then there is little need for trust. If either party cheats the other, the contract already spells out the penalty that will befall the bad guy in the deal. All of this requires costly negotiation, well-written and well-enforced laws, and lots of lawyers. In poor countries, trust and contracts-by-handshakes are an attractive lower-cost alternative.

Evidence: Civic Norms

Trust is only one aspect of the social cohesion triumvirate identified by Putnam and discussed in the previous chapter. Knack and Keefer's study investigates the relationship between economic growth and the other two aspects of social cohesion: norms and networks. To measure the extent of civic norms in a country, the authors used five questions from the World Values Survey. Survey respondents were asked whether the following actions can or cannot ever be justified:

- "claiming government benefits which you are not entitled to"
- "avoiding a fare on public transport"
- "cheating on taxes if you have the chance"
- "keeping money that you have found"

- "failing to report damage you've done accidentally to a parked vehicle"

From survey responses to these questions, the authors calculated the average score and used this index in their growth regressions. The international variation in the civic norms index is not as great as the variation in the rate of trust. The civic norms index has a positive and significant effect on economic growth rates; even when both the trust variable and the civic norms variable are included, both have a statistically significant and positive impact on growth. This suggests that norms and trust are not simply two ways of measuring the same thing, but distinct dimensions of social cohesion. If the norms index and the trust level merely measured the same underlying phenomenon, then if both were included in the same regression, one or both would cease to have a statistically significant effect on economic growth.

Knack and Keefer's analysis reveals some insights about the way in which trust and norms influence growth. Recall that the traditional sources of growth include increases in the availability of productive resources like workers and machines, and improvements in productivity: getting more workers and machines (known technically as "factor accumulation"), or getting more out of the same number of workers and machines (technically, "productivity growth"), creates more output. When they include the rate of investment — the share of GDP devoted to new machines, equipment, and buildings — trust and civic norms are no longer statistically significant. What that means is that the effect of trust and civic norms on growth is channelled through their effect on investment. Higher levels of trust and more co-operative norms of behaviour appear to favour factor accumulation, investment in productive physical capital. If trust and norms favoured productivity growth as well as factor accumulation, their effect would continue to be statistically significant when the investment rate is included in the regression.

This weak effect of social cohesion on productivity improvement is mirrored in work by University of British Columbia economist John Helliwell, who finds, in a study of seventeen high-income economies over the period 1962–1989, that an index of social cohesion (calculated based on World Values Survey data regarding trust, group memberships, and attitudes) is *negatively* related to productivity growth.

An alternative to measuring civic norms is to find measures of the civic engagement that those norms create. Putnam's study of Italy, indeed, emphasized the critical role of civic engagement, as did de Tocqueville 150 years before Putnam. In this connection, the cross-country growth study by Jonathan Temple and Paul A. Johnson (1998) is particularly useful. Temple and Johnson use a complicated index of "social capability" computed for many countries in 1960, and find that the index is positively and significantly related to subsequent growth. Social capability has a positive impact on growth even when the investment rate is included among the explanatory variables. This means that a nation's social capability, measured in this way, has an effect on growth independently of its effect on factor accumulation. Johnson and Temple's painstaking analysis of the components of the social-capability index uncovers the important role of mass-communications development (i.e., the penetration of radios and newspaper circulation) around 1960. This variable is not simply capturing the effect of income or literacy, given that those variables are also included. It could be that mass-communications development signals greater associational propensity; engaged, participatory citizens might demand more information about the workings of society; or conversely, greater availability of information about the doings of society might lead to more engaged, participatory citizens.

Evidence: Networks

Finally, Knack and Keefer also assess the contribution of associational life to growth. This is a surprising portion of their research, because it contradicts Putnam's findings in Italy, reviewed in Chapter 1. They include in yet another kitchen-sink regression the number of groups to which the average person belongs, also from the World Values Survey. This ranges from 0.38 in Japan to 1.7 in Iceland. The density of group membership turns out not to be related to growth rates at all. Of course, some groups might foster norms of co-operation and fellow feeling, as Putnam supposed they would, but other groups foster insularity and exclusiveness that is bad for the economy. That groups might be bad for the collective of the whole is an idea associated with the late economist Mancur Olson. Accordingly, Knack and Keefer add up what they consider to be positive, pro-social Putnamesque groups: religious or church organizations; education, arts, music, or cultural activities; youth work (e.g., scouts, guides, youth clubs), and they dub these P-groups. They separately add up harmful Olsonian groups — trade unions; political parties or groups; professional associations — and call them O-groups. Including people's tendency to be members of P-groups and O-groups in the statistical analysis does not help: O-group memberships have no effect, positive or negative, on growth or investment, while P-group memberships, perversely, are *negatively* related to investment.

Other research has contradicted this disappointing result regarding associational life. Furthermore, there are problems with the World Values Survey data on group memberships. For example, there is no measure of a person's degree of commitment to a group; this might be measured by the hours devoted to the group in a week, or the financial contributions she makes to the group. Furthermore, the data have been misinterpreted slightly. To be precise, the World Values Survey read a list of group *types* to survey respondents, and asked them whether they were members of a group of any of those types. Thus someone who was a member of five church-related groups, and no other groups, would have responded "yes" to the question about "religious or church organizations", and would have received a group-membership score of 1. Someone else, a member of, say, a trade union and a political party, would have answered yes to two group-type questions, and would receive a group-membership score of 2. Thus Knack and Keefer's group-membership score really measures the *diversity* of organizations to which an individual belongs, not the number of groups of which she is a member. In any case, in Chapter 3 we will review household-based studies that show a much stronger and positive relationship between households' associational life and their income levels.

Evidence: Responding to Shocks

There is at least one other arrow that leads from social cohesion to economic performance. Recall the "Backlash Hypothesis," first posited by Karl Polanyi in 1944 and enjoying renewed popularity in government circles in Canada and Europe: low social cohesion leads to social unrest of various stripes, all of which harm the prospects for economic growth. This is a qualitatively different story than one of trust or norms of civic engagement favouring economic exchanges; this is a political story that has adverse effects on the economy. One worry is that this will cause a backlash against even the putatively beneficial aspects of globalization.

Another arena where this kind of mechanism is likely to be at work is the problem of economic stabilization. The World Bank and the

International Monetary Fund have recommended a policy package of macroeconomic stabilization, including most notably exchange-rate devaluation and reduction of government budgets for unstable countries marked by high rates of inflation, foreign indebtedness, and trade deficits — ills that, by the way, frequently choke economic growth. Many economists, though they might quibble with the heavy-handed and anti-democratic nature of the imposition of these stabilization packages by the multilateral agencies, essentially agree with the fundamentals, just as they agree with the benefits of international economic integration. But a problem plagues these economists — if stabilization is good for people, why do right-thinking people in so many countries resist these measures for so long, only making the matter worse? Alberto Alesina and Allen Drazen (1991) theorized that the answer might lie in the degree of social cohesion in a country. They define social cohesion explicitly as the unevenness in the sharing of the burdens of stabilization. Where governments have a tendency to concentrate the benefits of growth among a small group of favoured individuals, some groups will quite rationally suspect that they will have to shoulder a disproportionate share of the burdens of stabilization. These burdens might include reduced government spending and rising prices for many essential goods. The lower the level of social cohesion, defined in this way, the longer the delay in implementing needed economic reform.

Parenthetically, influential Harvard University economist Dani Rodrik (1996) suggests that right-thinking people might resist these reforms because their track record is not so good. In particular, and simplifying his argument quite a bit, Rodrik demonstrates that the policies generally recommended by the World Bank — privatization, deregulation, liberalization of financial markets and international trade — have a mixed record in developing countries. Meanwhile, the policies generally recommended by the IMF — discipline in government spending and realistic exchange rates — have universally been associated with renewed growth.

Rodrik, indeed, in a 1998 statistical study of his own, illustrates the importance of social conflict, or the absence of social cohesion, and of the formal institutions of conflict resolution in society. Rodrik considers democratic institutions, an effective judiciary, a bureaucracy relatively free of corruption, and social insurance (like Employment Insurance and Medicare in Canada) to be indicators of effective institutions of conflict resolution. For social fragmentation he uses a series of indicators including income inequality (which will be the subject of Chapter 5) and "ethno-linguistic fragmentation," an ingenious index defined as the probability that any two people in a country chosen at random will not be members of the same ethno-linguistic group. He attempts to explain the *difference* in growth rates between the 1960–1975 period and the 1975–1990 period; for much of the world, increased oil prices and other shocks drastically reduced growth in the latter period.

Rodrik confirms that countries with greater latent social conflict and weaker institutions for conflict management fared worse in the latter period; indeed, once we account for those factors, government policies harped on by the World Bank and the IMF — government deficits and openness to international trade — have surprisingly small impacts. Rodrik's measures of social conflict do not change, of course, between the 1960–1975 and 1975–1990 periods: within countries, there are rarely sudden changes in the ethno-linguistic composition of the population. That means that the absence of cohesion in itself did not cause the growth slowdown. Rodrik's interpretation is that the presence of latent conflict determines a society's response to shocks from the world economy, and more fractured societies responded with less appropriate policies.

Unanswered Questions

Vast differences in average incomes among countries pose an unsolved puzzle for economics. Surely no country would "choose" an average income level equal to one-fortieth of the Canadian average. The standard economic model of growth signals rates of saving and of investment in education as critical determinants of a country's income level and growth rate, but savings rates and educational levels simply do not vary enough to explain the variation in living standards in the world today.

This chapter has illustrated that in the search for answers to this puzzle, new research indicates that loosely-defined concepts such as social capital, trust, or social capability might contribute to explaining those differences. Among the measures of social cohesion that researchers have included in their kitchen-sink regressions of growth performance are:

- the level of trust reported by people in a country
- the degree to which people subscribe to civic norms
- the degree to which people join organizations or perform volunteer work

- the extent of mass-communications development
- the existence of ethnic fragmentation and conflict.

The wealth of new studies on the topic has produced, as is typical in a new field of research, results that are not always comparable, commensurate, or consistent. But the preponderance of the evidence suggests that social cohesion, measured in the ways listed above, has a large and statistically significant relationship to economic growth.

How do these variables affect the economy? As a way of structuring one's understanding of this question, it is useful to recall that economic growth is always attributable to a combination of factor accumulation (especially investment in new machines and equipment), and productivity increases (the adoption of new technologies and ways of organizing production). To say that social cohesion favours growth is to say that it has some effect on factor accumulation or productivity growth or both. Some of the studies (notably those by Knack and Keefer, and by Helliwell) suggest that higher trust levels favour factor accumulation, but not necessarily productivity increases. This is consistent with our thought experiment regarding what would happen if everyone in Canada were as honest as Jason Fitzgerald of Halifax, Nova Scotia: the costs of business would be lower, and more new businesses would successfully secure start-up financing. Other studies, like Temple and Johnson's research into the effects of mass-communications development, demonstrate that social cohesion plays a role in productivity increases. Perhaps better channels of communication favour the dissemination of new techniques and practices. That trust appears to favour larger-scale firms similarly demonstrates the way that trust permits organizational innovations — in this case, large, lower-cost firms — that would otherwise be infeasible.

Still other studies claim that that social cohesion affects the economy only indirectly via its effect on political processes. This school of thought can be traced as least as far back as Putnam's research on regional governments in Italy; where the citizenry is more civically engaged, the government is better monitored and performs better as a result. Good government fosters better economic outcomes. Rodrik's finding that more cohesive societies better weather external economic shocks is consistent with this mechanism as well.

The research reviewed in this chapter has shown that, in international comparisons, social cohesion is a quantitatively and qualitatively important ingredient in the recipe for economic growth. This review of the research demonstrates, nevertheless, that there is no clear consensus about the specific route through which it works. Nor, indeed, is there clear consensus about exactly what social cohesion *is*. Of course, there is no need for unanimity among researchers and policy-makers regarding a single definition of social cohesion. But if, indeed, we care about social cohesion and its economic consequences, clarity in our thinking will aid policy-makers to craft more appropriate policies to preserve and promote social cohesion. Accordingly, the following chapters will clarify the macroeconomic trends reviewed in this chapter.

Bibliographic Notes

The debate regarding the US-Canada productivity gap is succinctly summarized in Sharpe (2000). Empirical research on the determinants of economic growth rates is summarized by Prescott (1998). The laudable exploits of the honest Haligonian are reported by Brooks (2000). The empirical research on social capital and growth is exhaustively summarized by Knack (1999), and by Temple (2000), from which this chapter has extensively drawn.

3

Co-operation and Social Cohesion in the Modern Economy

Former US President Ronald Reagan is reputed to have said that economists' stock-in-trade is to take things that work in practice and see if they work in theory. In the previous chapter, we saw suggestive macroeconomic evidence that various measures of social cohesion — trust, norms, and networks — are positively related to economic growth. In the Reagan formulation, then, social cohesion "works in practice"; in this chapter, we' will attempt to determine whether it works in theory as well.

In fairness, we are doing something more than just that. Based on the macroeconomic evidence in Chapter 2, a cautious and circumspect observer would note that one can only say certain measures of social cohesion are *positively associated* with economic growth: they do not necessarily *cause* that growth. This is one of the reasons social scientists, including economists, undertake theoretical work in the first place — to make sense of empirical observations. Moreover, the macroeconomic evidence looks at the statistical relationships among aggregates — total investment in a country, average trust in a country, economic growth in a country, enrolment ratios in a country, and so on. The unit of analysis is a nation. The knitted warmth that Buckler wrote about may be an asset upon which a nation can draw, but it is generated by the relationships among individual people. Therefore, to complement the aggregate focus of the previous chapter, this chapter will focus on the individual as the unit of analysis.

Specifically, this chapter will demonstrate the critical importance of co-operative behaviour to the liberal capitalist economy. It will then show how social cohesion can increase the level of co-operative behaviour so necessary to the functioning of the market system.

Co-operation and the Market Economy

In the early months of 2000, opposition Members of Parliament criticized the Liberal government for making job grants to firms that went bankrupt or went out of business shortly after receiving the grants. Prime Minister Jean Chrétien dismissed the notion that the grants had been poorly targeted with characteristic confidence. "[I]n a market economy, some people fail," he said, explaining helpfully that only in Communist countries is there a guarantee that no one goes broke.

We think we understand how the market-based, capitalist economy works, and many of us probably regard it as a cold and unforgiving system. As the Prime Minister duly noted, some people fail; that is the price we pay for the extraordinary dynamism and efficiency of the system. It is characteristic of this view that capitalism should be contrasted with communism, as the Prime Minister does. Since the fall of the Berlin Wall, of course, the viability of communism as an alternative to the current system, at least in North America, is not only a non-starter, but generally considered laughably unrealistic. (And it is certainly in this sense that Chrétien made his remarks.) Under capitalism, there is relentless competition; government regulation, to the extent that it is recommended, should merely safeguard and, indeed, enhance the competitiveness of markets.

This view of the capitalist economy in which we live, so prevalent in popular discourse, resembles the textbook economy that we teach in our economics classrooms. Firms battle with one another to produce goods at the lowest cost; workers compete for jobs. The only form of social interconnectedness is the price signal. The price of any good contains all you need to know about the production of that good. If you choose not to buy bread from a given baker, that in turn tells the baker something about the attractiveness of the price. That baker might not be able to compete with others. In market economies, some people fail. Of course, the wage paid by an employer is just another price: it tells the employee the money value of what she produces, and if she fails to produce commensurate value, she will be dismissed. In a market economy, some people fail. This cold-blooded calculus, nevertheless, roots out inefficiency and rewards innovation, delivering high volumes of production.

Equipped with this view of the market economy, it is difficult to see exactly how social cohesion could play a role, good or bad, in the smooth functioning of such a system. Employers provide workers with incentives to work hard via the wages that they pay. Consumers provide firms with incentives to be efficient via the prices they are willing to pay for various goods and services; this extends to inventors and entrepreneurs, who stand to profit from the consumer demand for the eventual fruits of their innovation. Trust, norms, and networks are superfluous. I need not trust my employee, because if he does anything untrustworthy, I will fire him. I need not trust my employer, because if she is untrustworthy, I will quit.

However, co-operation, it turns out, is critical to the functioning of the capitalist system. It is critical even in the rarefied realm of the textbook ideal, and it is even more critical to the working of the economy on the street, as it were: in real workplaces, in real markets. It is not the intention of this chapter to argue the superiority, whether moral or technical, of the capitalist mode of production, but rather to point out that the successful functioning of that system, even in the views of its most ardent supporters, is based on a network of co-operative behaviour and adherence to norms.

Social Cohesion in the Textbook Economy

Let us remain for a moment in the company of the ideal textbook market system. As noted above, the only kind of interaction among people in that system is the price mechanism: prices communicate scarcity and abundance of goods and services and guide people to make efficient decisions about what to consume and what to produce. Even this cold and stark network of interaction, however, presumes a backdrop of norms. For example, our textbooks assume that the household, in deciding what to purchase, is constrained by its own income. As economist Partha Dasgupta reminds us, there is an admittedly minimalist moral philosophy underlying that assumption: in the Hobbesian state of nature, a household could very well choose to broaden its consumption possibilities by expropriating, by violence, the incomes of other households. Indeed, this happens in the real world.

More generally, the textbook capitalist system relies on a modicum of well-observed contracts among buyers and sellers and workers and employers. Market-mediated exchange, even in a competitive setting, is more successful if buyers and sellers can be reasonably assured that they will not be ripped off by the other party. Exchanges that take place over time, like the granting of a loan in exchange for interest payments, or the delivery of goods to be paid for in the future, will not happen at all if there is no trust between the parties. Even those economists most resolutely opposed to the meddling of governments in the market system acknowledge the productive contribution of the monitoring and enforcement of laws regarding contracts and property. Writing such laws, revisiting and revising them from time to time, is a collective enterprise, even if it is carried out by an authoritarian king, because the resources needed to write, monitor, and enforce laws are provided by the community through their taxes.

From the earliest writers on the capitalist system, it has been recognized that obeying these laws that make markets work better is not solely a case of fearing punishment. In Canada today, for example, most people arguably follow many laws out of a sense of duty rather than an immediate fear of being detected and punished if they break the law. This is substantially different from the unbridled self-interest habitually associated with the capitalist economy. Adam Smith, the eighteenth-century political philosopher, declared, famously, that "[i]t is not from the benevolence of the butcher, the brewer, or the baker, that we expect our dinner, but from their regard to their own self interest." Less widely known, he also argued that:

> The regard to those general rules of conduct, is what is generally called a sense of duty, a principle of the greatest consequence in human life, and the only principle by which the bulk of mankind are capable of directing their actions ... Upon the tolerable observance of these duties depends the very existence of human society, which would crumble into nothing if mankind were not generally impressed with a reverence for those important rules of conduct.

So even the hard-boiled capitalist economy requires a legal framework and a tolerable observance of certain rules of conduct.

Real-World Markets and Social Cohesion

But the complicated translation of the textbook economy to the real world opens up an even more important role for social cohesion. The price mechanism cannot necessarily orchestrate all resource-allocation decisions in a complex economy. In such a context, non-market-mediated co-operation can assume a critical role in co-ordinating people's actions: different levels of social capital or social cohesion, given that they guide people's expectations about the behaviour of others, can provide co-ordination where the price mechanism cannot.

Take the example of a manufacturing firm. There are a multitude of tasks involved in putting together sophisticated products like automobiles. For a firm in a textbook, it might be feasible to contract separately for each of those tasks, every day. Monday, the firm hires an individual contractor to attach wheels to the chassis of the car, it hires another to attach windshields, it hires another to attach brake lights, and so on. Someone else is hired to do the accounting on Monday, someone else is hired to clean the floors. Tuesday morning the firm decides how much of each of these services it will require, and hires a bunch more independent contractors for the day. Some of the same people might be hired, although maybe not. For each contract, the firm pays precisely the incremental value of the service provided to the firm. Only workers with the requisite skills will be able to fill each of these positions; lower-skilled contractors will get lower payments for the services they provide (which, after all, require lower skills). Higher-skilled workers only accept highly-paid contracts because they could demand high payment for work provided to other firms.

This is a bit of a caricature, but it resembles the workings of the textbook economy much more closely than it does the economy where we really live. In practice, for example, the cost of rehiring the entire workforce every day is prohibitive in the automobile industry. Of course there are exceptions: in poor agrarian economies in the developing world (and indeed, historically, in Canada), workers are often hired on a daily basis for physically-demanding tasks. With the advent of lower-cost communications technology, manufacturing firms can "source" the lowest cost components, switching rapidly among suppliers. Nevertheless, for a host of important tasks, the firm will hire relatively long-term employees to perform a number of tasks. Now the wage paid to the worker is not an exact signal of the value of, say, attaching four wheels to a car on the assembly line; it is a sort of average of the value to the firm of a number of different tasks. Moreover, it is an imprecise average since frequently neither the firm nor the worker knows precisely which tasks will be required at the time the worker is hired.

There is a further complication. When our textbook automobile manufacturer hires an army of independent contractors, it presumably can monitor the quantity and quality of work done by each of them — after all, it is essentially paying piece rates like eighteenth-century textile manufacturers in England. In the real world, there is considerable uncertainty about how assiduously the employee is working at all times, and it is not always simple or costless to monitor his or her progress. In situations of team production the individual worker's contribution to output might be impossible to measure. Furthermore, there will likely always remain some important dimensions of the worker's effort that cannot be easily monitored. This is particularly important where workers' performance is highly interrelated. One worker's shirking has consequences that ripple through the production chain. Five years from now, if a wheel comes flying off a car barrelling down the highway, it would be very difficult to pin the blame on negligence on the part of our automobile-factory worker; many other people's actions have impinged on the car in the meantime, from co-workers to dealers to mechanics to the owner. Accordingly, economists believe that when monitoring of employees is difficult and expensive, employers will use wages as a disciplinary device. One of the consequences is that people will be paid slightly more than the market-clearing wage — the wage that equates supply and demand for labour of that level of skill. This, in turn, will mean that some people at that skill level are unable to find work at the going wage; those lucky enough to secure jobs will be careful not to jeopardize their good fortune by malfeasance, nonfeasance or misfeasance at work. Alternative theories view this ever-so-slightly high wage not so much as a threat — screw up, and you'll lose this good thing — as a gift from the employer, for which he expects the employee to "go the extra mile."

That employees sometimes do "go the extra mile" is illustrated quite clearly by the effectiveness of the "work-to-rule" threat in labour disputes. Unions — like the pilots' union in Canada in the summer of 2000 — threaten that they will "work-to-rule": essentially, that they will do everything they are contractually obliged to do, and no more. Obviously, the contract must not specify all the things that workers do as a matter of course, or this would not be a potent threat. In labour markets where "work-to-rule" is a feared and costly threat, workers and managers are certainly engaged in an economic relationship where social cohesion plays an important role.

(Many readers might be nonplussed to learn that economists think of wages as "too high" in any sense. Wages are conceived of as high only in the sense that there are people out there seeking work who cannot find it, and if prevailing wages were to fall from their current levels, it is more likely that firms would hire them.)

Consider what the beleaguered wage is expected to do. In the textbook, the wage is merely a price signal, which, under ideal circumstances, is meant to equate the worker's cost of time — she could be working at the next-best job, or enjoying free time — and the value of her work to the employer. In reality, where labour turnover and monitoring workers are costly for the firm, the wage signals the worker's cost of time, as well as the value attached by the employer to her work; but it also serves to discipline workers, or imbue them with a warm glow toward their bosses; and it is meant to reflect the average value of a large number of tasks undertaken by the worker and not necessarily known when she is hired. This is a lot to ask of a single number like ten dollars an hour. Market relationships between employers and workers are especially susceptible to the effects of trust, or its absence. So too are the relationships between firms and consumers, or among firms themselves. This class of problems has been extensively studied under the heading of "the prisoners' dilemma," to which we now turn.

The Prisoners' Dilemma

Trust and co-operative behaviour are salient features of economic interactions in rich and poor countries alike. Nevertheless the role of trust is qualitatively different at different stages of development. In South Asia and sub-Saharan Africa, the poorest regions of the world, fewer than ten percent of the population lives in cities of more than one million inhabitants; in high-income countries, a third of the people live in such cities (World Bank, 2000). At the level of economic development of South Asia and sub-Saharan Africa, many, perhaps most, interactions occur between people who know each other, and reputations influence economic transactions. Kinship relations or common membership in political parties or religious organizations overlap with economic transactions. These personal networks can be exploited to make the system of economic exchange work more smoothly. Group-lending or "microfinance" schemes to alleviate rural poverty, like the justly celebrated Grameen Bank in Bangladesh, attempt to do just that.

In contrast, when people interact in large cities, anonymity is the rule in a far larger number of interactions and economic transactions. There is no particular history underlying a random encounter between two strangers. If one is a buyer and another a seller, there is likely no other relationship between the two, unlike the familial and social linkages that would loom behind the commercial transaction in a small village, or even in the medieval city with its self-enclosed guilds and clans. That is not to say that there is no information underlying the interaction. It may appear miraculous that one stranger agrees to hand over voluntarily hundreds of dollars worth of merchandise to another, who has merely displayed a credit card to the former; the existence of a data base with the stranger's credit history ensures the buyer's reputation for honesty is in fact considered, despite the anonymity of the transaction. Nevertheless, even anonymous transactions in large cities occur in the shadow of society-wide expectations regarding trust and co-operative behaviour. The relative balance between reputation-driven and anonymous interactions differs across rich and poor countries, between rural and urban societies: both information-rich and information-poor social interactions will be analyzed in this chapter.

In many of these social interactions, a person faces very strong incentives to exploit another person for personal reward, even though mutual co-operation is better for all parties. This is the quandary of the so-called *prisoners' dilemma* in economic theory. In one of the classic statements of the problem, economists R. Duncan Luce and Howard Raiffa wrote in 1957 (p. 95):

> Two suspects are taken into custody and separated. The district attorney is certain that they are guilty of a specific crime, but he does not have enough adequate evidence to convict them at a trial. He points out to each prisoner that each has two alternatives: to confess to the crime the police are sure they have done, or not to confess. If they both do not confess, then the district attorney states he will book them on some very minor trumped-up charge such as petty larceny and illegal possession of a weapon, and they will both receive minor punishment; if they both confess they will be prosecuted, but he will recommend less than the most severe sentence; but if one confesses and the other does not, then the confessor will receive lenient treatment for turning state's evidence whereas the latter will get "the book" slapped at him.

(This statement of the problem is redolent of the US criminal-justice system, but I trust that Canadian readers are sufficiently inundated with crime shows from American television that they are completely conversant with the idiom.) Clearly, the prisoners isolated in separate interrogation rooms would be jointly best off if neither confessed: between them, they would do very little jail time. There is no collective dilemma, then: the best course of action is clear. The dilemma is present for each prisoner *individually*. Say that the prisoners are Bonnie and Clyde (to continue with the "lawless Americans" theme). It is critical to assume in what follows that "lenient treatment" is better than "minor punishment." Bonnie thinks to herself that Clyde will either confess or not. If he confesses and Bonnie does not, then Bonnie will get the book thrown at her (in this hard-boiled argot, I believe the book is "thrown," not "slapped," but we can forgive a pair of 1950s game theorists their less than perfect fluency); if she also confesses, her punishment will be less than "the book." If Clyde does *not* confess and Bonnie does not confess, her punishment will be minor; if she confesses in this instance, however, she will do even better, receiving lenient treatment. What does this mean? Whether Clyde confesses or not, it is always best for Bonnie to confess. (A key component of this situation is that each makes a decision without knowing what the other is doing, which is more or less like saying that they choose their strategies simultaneously.) The problem is entirely symmetrical, and Clyde can go through the same mental process and decide that, no matter what happens, he should also confess. In the parlance of game theory, "confess" is a dominant strategy for each player, and the predicted outcome is that both will confess, even though both would be better off if neither confessed.

The relevance of the prisoners' dilemma to economics is that many social interactions in markets that fail to meet the textbook ideal have the character of this conundrum facing Bonnie and Clyde. The usual invisible-hand logic of economics, since Adam Smith in 1776, suggests that self-interested people making decisions in a de-centralized fashion will reach a general equilibrium that is also a social optimum. In the prisoners' dilemma we have a case where the equilibrium (our prediction regarding what will occur) is not the social optimum (the most-desirable alternative among all possible outcomes). This is a dispiriting outcome for fans of the optimality of decentralized decision making.

The prisoners' dilemma rears its head in various economic guises. The so-called "Tragedy of the Commons" afflicts users of com-monly-owned natural resource systems, like an inshore fishery or a village pasture in the following way. If I overfish, it imposes a cost on all other users of the fishery; other fishermen must search longer, at greater cost, for relatively fewer fish. Moreover, overfishing im-poses a dynamic cost on others, in that it increases the probability that the fishery will be decimated forever. Clearly, the social opti-mum is for all of us to exercise restraint: we can all harvest fish at a lower unit cost, and we will all enjoy the benefits of the fishery for a longer time. However, if everyone else exercises restraint, I am tempted to overfish. If all my neighbours are overfishing, I gain nothing by exercising restraint. Overfishing is a dominant strategy, and the equilibrium prediction is that the fishery will be driven to extinction, a prediction all too sadly observed here in Canada.

Airplane mechanics, all else equal, probably find it tiresome to exert a high level of effort all the time, even though doing so is better for airline passengers, and for the mechanics themselves, to the extent that they benefit from the safety performance of the airline. Given the highly interrelated nature of what airplane mechanics do, it is best for the airline's owners and workers (and, not incidentally, its passengers) if the mechanics all exert a high level of effort at all times. But if everyone else is working hard, the individual mechanic has an incentive to rely on the hard work of others, not working so hard himself. And if no one else is working hard, the individual mechanic has even less incentive to work hard.

More generally, in many situations where co-operative behaviour by all leads to a social optimum, rational individuals face strong incentives to "defect" from the co-operative code of conduct. Organizing a citizens' movement of some kind requires hard work; I'd like to see the group succeed, but if everyone else does his or her part, I will still benefit from their efforts. Examples of this kind include neighbourhood-watch programs or volunteering activities. This suggests that civic engagement of the kind championed by the social cohesion research is likely to suffer from defection in the manner of the prisoners' dilemma.

To simplify the exposition, let us assign numerical payoffs to each player in a generic prisoners' dilemma. Suppose that our two players are again Bonnie and Clyde, and that each chooses between two strategies: co-operate or defect. Then there are four possible outcomes: mutual co-operation, mutual defection, and two mixed outcomes where one player co-operates and the other defects. Figure 3.1 summarizes this discussion.

In each of the four outcomes in Figure 3.1, Clyde's payoff is listed first and Bonnie's is second. Thus, if Bonnie defects and Clyde co-operates, Bonnie earns a payoff of 3 and Clyde earns a payoff of -1. We suppose that each player's objective is to earn the highest possible payoff, and assume that the payoffs are denominated in units of "utility," the conventional economic measure of happiness. Mutual co-operation yields the highest total payoff: 2 + 2 = 4, while

Figure 3.1: The Prisoners' Dilemma

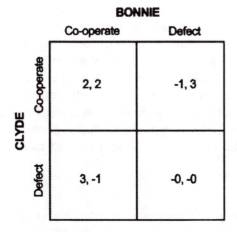

Note: In each cell, Clyde's payoff is listed first, Bonnie's second.

mutual defection yields a total payoff of zero. This simple depiction of the game also demonstrates each player's incentive to defect no matter what the other player does. Take Bonnie: if Clyde co-operates, she earns 3 by defecting, and 2 by co-operating; if Clyde defects, she earns 0 by defecting, which is better than -1 from co-operating. We will return to this simple depiction of the prisoners' dilemma in a moment.

The prisoners' dilemma is noteworthy not only for its prevalence in social interactions, but because it features a two-sided incentive problem: both Bonnie and Clyde are strongly dissuaded by circumstances from co-operating with each other. Many other types of strategic interaction might exhibit only one-sided opportunism of this type. Consider the relationship between a lender and borrower: if the borrower is protected by limited liability, she might face a strong temptation to abscond with the loan and not repay — that is, to "defect." Another example is the relationship between a corporation's board of directors and its management: the former would like the latter to maximize shareholder value, but the latter might have other objectives like building an internal empire and hiring close friends.

Sometimes the prisoners' dilemma is an accurate analytical framework. Fish species disappear, airplanes crash, people opt not to join a neighbourhood watch program or volunteer at their children's school, even though everyone agrees these outcomes are undesirable. At the same time, nevertheless, around the world, people in resource-using communities join together to voluntarily regulate their use of the commons, often meeting with great success. Hundreds of airplanes safely reach their destinations everyday. Some neighbourhoods enjoy safe streets through the engagement of the people who live there; some schools have lots of parent involvement. It is the contention of this chapter that social cohesion is a useful framework for understanding why co-operative outcomes sometimes emerge and endure. Social cohesion changes the incentives facing people and helps groups of rational decision-makers avoid the ills of massive defection.

Social Capital

This book has progressed quite a long way without bothering to precisely define concepts like social capital, social cohesion, or community, despite their centrality to the discussion so far. Social capital means different things to different people. Indeed, it sometimes means different things to the *same* people.

Political scientist Robert Putnam, whose work on Italy was reviewed in Chapter 1, sees social capital as those "features of social organization, such as trust, norms, and networks, that can improve the efficiency of society by facilitating coordinated actions" (1993, p. 167). Sociologist James Coleman, meanwhile, declares that "social capital inheres in the structure of relations between persons and among persons. It is lodged neither in individuals nor in physical implements of production" (1990, p. 302). The macroeconomic studies reviewed in Chapter 2 likewise see social capital as a characteristic of the economy as a whole. Pierre Bourdieu's definition echoes these society-wide concerns, while also emphasizing agents' information about each other: social capital is "the aggregate of the actual or potential resources which are linked to possession of a durable network of more or less institutionalized relationships of mutual acquaintance and recognition — or in other words, to membership in a group — which provides each of its members with the backing of the collectively-owned capital" (1986, p. 249). Francis Fukuyama defines social capital as "society's stock of shared values" and "a set of informal values or norms shared among members of a group that permits cooperation among them" (1999, pp. 14, 16).

There are important fundamental distinctions among these differing definitions. Is social capital something that inheres in the individual, or a characteristic of a group of people? I will argue that social capital is best understood as being similar to human capital. Human capital is an individual characteristic: it is the total amount of education and training that you have acquired, and it increases your productivity (and hence your earning power). The nation's stock of human capital is just the aggregate value of education and training, adding up for all individuals. In practice, an economy's human-capital stock is frequently estimated by looking at the number of school-age children enrolled in school, or the percentage of the adult population that can read and write. (Whether *physical* capital inheres in the individual or the economy at large is an even less complicated question. If you buy a lathe, it is yours. Period.) So, too, social capital is a characteristic, an asset, of the individual.

Nevertheless, neither human capital nor social capital can be effectively analysed by looking at the individual in isolation. People's decisions about whether or not to acquire human capital are interrelated. The higher the level of human capital of my co-worker, the higher the return to my own investments in human capital; conversely, my investments in human capital redound to the benefit of my co-workers and others in the economy. These interrelationships provide a strong basis for mandatory schooling, given that people would not necessarily take into account the benefits of their schooling for other people when making investments in human capital. (Similarly, people's decisions about whether to invest in physical capital are interrelated: the higher the rate at which others are investing, the higher the return to me from investing. This provides a justification for public investment that is analogous to the justification for publicly-funded universal education.)

Social capital is perhaps more ephemeral than human capital, but its relationship to the individual and society as a whole is fundamentally similar. People make social-capital investments — they volunteer their time to a community organization or political party or soccer club. From this they derive the benefit of the social contacts they make. These networks may serve economic ends in a highly formalized way. In many developing countries, people in agrarian villages or urban neighbourhoods join groups that essentially act like insurance companies, paying in during relatively good times, and making withdrawals when hit by some economic calamity. Alternatively, the rationale of the groups may not be so expressly economic, as is the case of choral societies. Nevertheless, Putnam's work in Italy shows that even singing groups seem to contribute to better government efficiency (which in turn leads to better economic performance).

Social-capital investments change the incentives facing people. In the best of cases, they transform prisoners' dilemmas into situations where people are better off co-operating.

One example where the co-ordinating role of social capital or social cohesion can make a difference in economic outcomes is the problem of the commons mentioned above. One person's restraint in using the resource provides benefits for other members of the resource-using community, but her neighbours do not pay her for conserving. The fleeting nature of many common-pool resources, like irrigation water or migratory species, makes it difficult to establish perfect property rights in those resources, and consequently the price mechanism assigns no price to conservation. All else equal, each person has an incentive to over-exploit the resource, because she does not take into account the benefit her restraint provides to others.

More concretely, consider the Mexican farmer-managed irrigation systems I visited (and described in Chapter 1). Similar irrigation communities are widespread in the developing world. Every year, farmers must clean the canal network to increase the flow of irrigation water. But this problem bears a strong family resemblance to the prisoners' dilemma, given that canal cleaning creates positive spillovers for other irrigators. One farmer may choose not to exert tedious effort cleaning a stretch of the canal, instead free-riding off the effort of his neighbour. But if all farmers think in this way, the equilibrium outcome might be entirely uncleaned canals, and lower water flows for all. (Strictly speaking, the costs of uncleaned canals, realized in the form of lower output, will not be equally borne, as those farmers at the end of the canal network will suffer the accumulated effects of clogged canals. Nevertheless, all farmers depend on the cleanliness of the main canal that links the water source (reservoir, well, river diversion) to the field channels, and even the first farmer to divert water suffers from the failure of collective canal cleaning.) This in turn creates a private loss for all farmers, since their crop yields are lower. What I observed in Mexico, and what political scientist Elinor Ostrom (1990) and others have shown, is that community investments in rules to manage the commons can transform payoffs of the prisoners' dilemma game. As a result, mutual co-operation — high levels of canal cleaning, with concomitant high crop yields and incomes — becomes an equilibrium outcome.

What is social capital? If one farmer attends the annual meeting of the irrigation society, he incurs a cost in time and perhaps tedium. The outcome of the meeting, however, is the co-ordination of canal cleaning and irrigation-water delivery among all those who attended. If our farmer and his neighbours follow the plan settled upon in the meeting, their individual returns to co-operation — in the form of their profits from the crops they grow — are higher than they would have been without the meeting. Attending a meeting signals a player's willingness to co-operate in the future by raising the payoff she receives from being co-operative. Her payoff is raised by learning about the co-ordination of canal-cleaning. If she adheres to the canal cleaning plan, the return to her co-operative effort will be higher — her co-operative effort would have a very low return if instead she opted to clean the canal six months before irrigation was to begin, or two days *after* it began. Furthermore, since her payoff as well as everyone else's increases as she increases her canal-cleaning effort, her payoff increases with her social-capital investment.

Alternatively, return to the example of the airplane mechanic. The co-operation decision facing two aircraft-maintenance workers is whether to provide a high effort level or to shirk. The management cannot perfectly observe the level of effort provided. All else being equal, both would prefer to shirk, even given the monetary and monitoring incentives provided by the management. If both shirk, it substantially increases the probability that the aircraft will suffer some kind of mishap, reducing the long-term income of both workers if the company goes out of business as a result. But suppose, in this simple setting, that both workers have the option of attending a purely voluntary training session prior to working on the plane. If the first mechanic goes to the training session and sees the second there, it increases his expectation that the second mechanic will not shirk. If the training session imparts information that raises both workers' productivity when they provide high effort subsequently, so much the better. This in turn further reduces the risk of accidents, thereby increasing the firm's success and the lifetime income of the mechanics.

The stock of social capital in an economy is the sum of these investments at a given time for all people in the economy. Like human capital, people's decisions about investing in social capital are interrelated. The more my neighbours invest, the higher the return to my own social-capital investment. The greater the effort expended by my co-workers, the greater the return to participating in on-the-job training programs. In the parlance of economics, there are strong *strategic complementarities* in social-capital investment: the level of your investment and the level of my investment are complementary. Social capital is not entirely analogous to physical or human capital: a player only realizes the return to social-capital investment if mutual co-operation occurs. In fact, this is a practical economic definition of social capital: like all investments, it yields a return, but that return only happens if people co-operate.

What makes social-capital investment more likely? The larger the return to mutual co-operation, the more likely that universal investment will constitute a focal point for people. For village irrigators, a high rate of return means that the relationship between co-ordination efforts and increased water supply is very pronounced. For airplane mechanics, a high rate of return means that the information imparted at the training session is especially productive in reducing airplane crashes, but relies critically on co-ordinated effort among the mechanics. If the return to unilaterally defecting when your neighbour or co-worker co-operates is very small, this will also make high levels of social capital investment more likely. One village irrigator elects not to clean his stretch of the canal network, benefiting from his neighbour's canal-cleaning effort, but the return is not great, perhaps because his opponent's effort provides little benefit for our defector. (This might be the case if little of the water that flows to the potential free rider does so through canals cleaned by his neighbour.) Or, for the airplane mechanics, failing to match one's co-worker's high effort level results in only a negligible increase in well-being derived from saved effort.

In a setting where people can make social-capital investments, the economic theory now predicts that mutual co-operation might be observed in equilibrium, even in difficult settings like the commons or the workplace.

Social Cohesion

It is useful to distinguish an individual's social-capital activity from the level of social-capital activity that is general in the society at large. What does this distinction mean? In terms of the simple model of social capital suggested above, suppose that a person takes a flight from a society with low social capital, like Nova Scotia, to one with high social capital, like Manitoba. (The choice of these particular place names is inspired by Table 1.4 on associational activity in the Canadian provinces.) The traveller is unlikely to have made many social-capital investments in his home province, given that so few other people have. But when he arrives in Manitoba, despite the fact that he is exactly the same person, with the same psychology and the same preferences, he is more likely to make social-capital investments there than in Nova Scotia. Nothing intrinsic to our traveller has changed, but there is something different about his new economic environment. In addition to social capital, which like lathes or education, is a characteristic of individuals, there is also some explicitly societal variable that matters here. This is what I have chosen to call *social cohesion*. This captures something in some of the definitions of social capital reviewed above; for example, the sociologist Coleman locates social capital in the "structure of relations," not in individuals.

The distinction between social capital and social cohesion can be illustrated by a simple economic model. Suppose that the economy comprises a large number of people and that all economic interactions are bilateral transactions that take the form of the prisoners' dilemma in Figure 3.1. This economy is more accursed than most real economies, given that *every* interaction here is marked by two-sided incentives toward defection; in real economies, many economic interactions have to deal only with incentives to defect for one player, or for neither. Now suppose that people in this economy are randomly matched in pairs to play the game in Figure 3.1. Then one well-founded prediction for this society is that mutual defection will mark every pairing of people.

But now let us suppose that each randomly-matched pair of people in this society, before playing the prisoners' dilemma game, has the opportunity to invest in something called "social capital." That is, before playing the game in Figure 3.1, both players simultaneously decide whether or not to invest in social capital, and once they have made their choices, each knows what the other chose. In fact, suppose that the social-capital investment requires a sacrifice of one unit of utility (one "util," in the parlance of textbook economics). That means that each player's payoff will be one unit less than the numbers given in Figure 3.1, if he or she makes this investment. Like any investment, however, it could pay off: we assume that it yields a return of two utils, but *only in the instance where both players co-operate in the prisoners' dilemma*. Then, if both players invest, and both subsequently co-operate, the payoffs are 3 for each player. (Each would have received 2 without the investment, but each sacrifices 1 for the social-capital investment; if both co-operate, they get

Figure 3.2: The Prisoners' Dilemma Modified

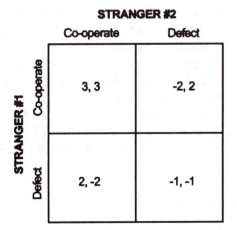

Note: In each cell, Stranger #1's payoff is listed first, Stranger #2's second.

2 additional units: 2 - 1 + 2 = 3.) In any other outcome of the prisoners' dilemma, the payoffs are simply reduced by one unit for each player. Thus, within our model economy, if a pair of people each make a social-capital investment visible to the other, then the prisoners' dilema is modified in the following way.

This changes things for our archetypal Strangers #1 and #2. If Stranger #2 defects, Stranger #1's best strategy is still to defect also: he gets -2 from co-operating and -1 from defecting. But if Stranger #1 suspects that Stranger #2 is going to co-operate, his best response is to co-operate as well: he gets 3 from co-operating and 2 from defecting. The problem is symmetrical, so Stranger #2 reasons similarly. Now, mutual defection is still an equilibrium outcome of this game, but it is no longer a dominant-strategy equilibrium; mutual co-operation is also a possible equilibrium outcome of this modified game. And there are reasons to suspect that mutual co-operation is more likely: after all, both players invested in social capital that would only pay off if they both co-operated. Why else did they make that sacrifice if they did not plan to co-operate once it came time to play the prisoners' dilemma? In this case, a reasonable prediction of conventional economics would be that widespread co-operation would emerge among many or most of the randomly-paired players in this model economy.

Now let us suppose that this game is not played just once, but that after the first round, the players are shuffled around and randomly matched again. Each player must once again decide whether to bother making an investment in social capital before playing the prisoners' dilemma game against her new partner. Once again, we would predict that many players would co-operate after all. But now change the set-up of the game as follows. The payoff to mutual co-operation, if both players invest in social capital, is no longer two utils, but rather some arbitrary rate of return that depends on society's history of co-operative behaviour. The more social-capital investment that has occurred in the past, the higher the rate of return to mutual co-operation today. Why might this be the case?

Consider again the example of village irrigation, but now let the growing season be repeated year after year. Then this set-up says that the payoff from co-ordinating canal-cleaning efforts and other tasks is higher in villages that have tended to undertake such co-ordination efforts in the past. As a village gets better at the complex task of collective management of its common asset, it becomes more profitable for each individual farmer to attend the yearly meeting and learn about the irrigation plan. Concretely, it might be that the meetings go more quickly, or that the collective becomes more efficient at allocating labour or making group decisions. More generally, the "habit" of reaching consensus is a group skill that must be learned. Over time, a group becomes more skilled in collective deliberations.

In the example of the airplane mechanics, over time our mechanics become more capable of assimilating information at training sessions. As a result, the session organizers can provide more information at each year's session. Moreover, the increased transmission of information translates into ever smaller probabilities of air accidents and ever higher lifetime earnings for the mechanics, should they elect not to shirk. More generally, consider firms' attempts to instill a "corporate culture" in their workplaces. Suppose that the aircraft-maintenance firm wished to inculcate a culture of "going the extra mile." For example, does a mechanic drop his tools immediately when the five-o'clock whistle blows, or does he stay a few minutes (or more) to finish the job "right"? Such choices are observable by other employees, though not necessarily by management. Firm-sponsored voluntary activities like training sessions (e.g., company picnics, softball games) can serve as opportunities for workers to signal to one another their intention to "go the extra mile"; in aircraft maintenance, the return to one worker's decision to do so is highly dependent on the probability that other workers will similarly be conscientious.

Consider the model with a changing payoff to mutual co-operation. And suppose that all anyone knows about economic conditions when she is matched up randomly with another player is the rate of return to mutual co-operation. She knows nothing about her partner this time around, about his history of co-operation. All she knows is the payoff for co-operators, something driven by the history of co-operation in her society. If this payoff is sufficiently high, then it is more likely that she (and her counterpart) will invest in social capital and co-operate when they play the prisoners' dilemma. And given the assumptions we have made, the more that people invest in social capital, the higher that rate of return will be, further encouraging social-capital investment and co-operation in the future. Mutual defection will become less and less likely as the payoff from co-operation grows. Such a society finds itself in a virtuous cycle. Given that co-operation contributes to, indeed, defines, economic performance, this high-social-cohesion economy will have better economic growth than would otherwise be the case.

Our examples of the airplane mechanics and irrigators suggested that the payoff to co-operation is, in part, monetary. Farmers in an irrigation community with a history of co-operation will have higher crop yields; fishermen in a fishing community with a history of co-operation will have higher fishing yields at a lower cost. Airplane mechanics and others in workplaces with a high level of social cohesion will be more productive, and consequently, better-paid. But of course the "return" to social-capital investment is more generally earned in terms of economic utility, which is ultimately psychological. More money will probably make a person economically happier, but non-monetary factors pay off too. If there are norms of co-operation, a person feels bad if he defects and good if he co-operates, aside from other considerations. Recall the case of Jason Fitzgerald from Chapter 2, who found and returned $1,000 worth of toonies. His rationale for his honest action is worth repeating here: "I work with kids and I try to instill good values in them ... It wouldn't be right if I were to turn around and do something like that." His civic engagement — a form of social-capital investment — raised the psychological payment to being honest. One thousand dollars is still one thousand dollars, but Fitzgerald's act of honesty provided some countervailing psychological satisfaction: he could derive utility from the example he provided to the children with whom he works.

Alternatively, had he kept the money, he would have benefited monetarily, but he would have felt bad, because he had acted against an internalized norm regarding appropriate behaviour.

Finally, the community irrigators and airplane mechanics are somewhat misleading examples, because the simple model of social cohesion would work among a population of strangers. Indeed, much of the policy attention to the ravelling of social cohesion is likely concerned with the mechanisms that lead total strangers to trust one another. People who know each other have additional advantages favouring co-operation. One might say that they have "community."

Community

Much of the discourse on social capital and social cohesion emphasizes the importance of community. Community enhances social capital and social cohesion, according to the World Bank, for example. Or perhaps social capital and social cohesion generate stronger communities. All of this begs the question of what *community* is. The *Merriam-Webster Dictionary* provides several definitions, among them:

- "a unified body of individuals, as a state, commonwealth"; "a body of persons or nations having a common history or common social, economic, and political interests"
- "an interacting population of various kinds of individuals (as species) in a common location"; "the people with common interests living in a particular area, broadly the area itself"; "a group of people with a common characteristic or interest living together within a larger society"
- "common character, likeness"; "social activity, fellowship"; "joint ownership or participation."

Two themes run through these various definitions. First, there is a merely descriptive idea of community: people living in a particular area, or the area itself, an interacting population. Second, there is a more idealistic view of community, characteristics that will not necessarily be exhibited by all interacting populations of geographically proximate individuals: unity, fellowship, likeness, common interests. There are furthermore many possible levels of the second, idealistic perspective of community. The Government of Canada's Policy Research Sub-Committee on Social Cohesion defines social cohesion as "the ongoing process of developing a community of shared values, shared challenges and equal opportunity." Rosell (1999) meanwhile, defines cohesion in relation to "shared communities of interpretation." Without necessarily adhering too closely to those authors' use of the terms, it is worth noting that a community of shared values implies a greater degree of common character than a community of interpretation. To take a rather homely example, workers and managers may have a common understanding of the process of wealth creation, a process that they all understand to involve the contribution of capital and labour; they have a community of interpretation. Nevertheless, workers may feel that management is appropriating an inappropriately large share of the gains from their joint production, an interpretation not shared by managers, and this disagreement may lead to strikes and other conflicts; the parties do not have a community of shared values. Alternatively, one could envision a setting — in a very hierarchical society, or in one where wages are struck in a corporatist framework, like the Scandinavia of yore — in which workers and managers share a community of interpretation regarding wealth creation, but also a community of shared values regarding the appropriate division of gains from the production process.

This book leans toward the idealistic, rather than descriptive, view of community, and attempts to blend the aspects of interpretation and values. Start with the society of total strangers analyzed in the light of social cohesion above. Formally, say that "community" exists when two additional conditions are met. First, in contrast to the basic social-cohesion game, where people know only the current level of social cohesion (i.e., the rate of payoff to mutual co-operation), in a community people have "good" information about each others' actions. This is the "mutual acquaintance and recognition" that form the core of Bourdieu's (1986) definition of social capital. Thus one player matched with another to play the prisoners' dilemma is not a total stranger to the other; in particular, a person likely knows something about whether or not her counterpart has co-operated or defected in the past. This is in the spirit of the "community of interpretation." Second, the group has a social standard of behaviour — a set of informal rules that promote co-operation and reciprocity. This reflects the collective's "community of shared values." Together, the information structure and the social standard of behaviour can be viewed as a social norm.

Let us enrich the social cohesion model developed above, to illustrate what makes a "community" distinct. First, the players are no longer complete strangers. Let's make a very weak assumption about the information that people have about one another. Assume that each player knows just one thing about the history of co-operative behaviour in society: he knows only if he has ever observed defection. This means only that he can remember whether anyone, including himself, that he has ever encountered during all of his randomly matched interactions, has ever chosen to defect during the prisoners' dilemma. Note that although this is not a lot of information, in the social-cohesion game above players did not even have this much knowledge about each other. For each interaction, their choices during the prisoners' dilemma were based solely on whether their current counterparts had invested in social capital; their strategies were not conditioned by any past observation of defection.

The second component of community given in our definition is the presence of a social standard of behaviour. Let us define a very simple rule of thumb for players in our model community. Suppose that the social standard of behaviour is this: invest in some social capital during your first random matching, and co-operate if your counterpart has also made a social-capital investment; thereafter, continue to invest in social capital and co-operate during each subsequent random matching, as long as no one (including yourself) that you encounter ever defects; if anyone ever defects, never invest in social capital again, and always defect thereafter. If everyone adheres to this social standard of behaviour, it is likely that the community will enjoy social capital investments and co-operation by all every round. The special characteristic of this social standard of behaviour is that if everyone else adheres to it, it pays me to adhere to it, too; in this way it enforces co-operative behaviour. Lurking in the background is disillusionment. If, under this social standard of behaviour, a member of an irrigating community ever discovers that one of her neighbours has failed to clean his assigned stretch of the canal system, she becomes disillusioned. Since she knows that most everyone hews to this social standard of behaviour, it is only a matter of time before someone else sees some evidence of defection, and before long everyone will be defecting every round. She will consequently never clean her segment of the public canal network again, and moreover she will cease to attend the annual assemblies of the irrigation community. If our airplane mechanic ever discovers that one of his colleagues has shirked once, he will become disillusioned with his workplace community as well. Knowing that everyone else will defect once they see defection, he reckons that he might as well start defecting today. He will never attend another training session, and he will shirk forever more, whatever the consequences are for travellers on the carrier or the firm that employs him. Moreover, it is a fragile equilibrium, in the sense that a single deviation — which never happens in the "good" equilibrium — sets off a chain of deviations that eventually engulf the whole community.

Real norms in real societies are considerably more complicated. But one important way in which they differ from this "contagion" standard is that they rely on much more information among the players. More information can only help, in that it opens up possibilities for more nuanced social norms, which can in turn more readily turn prisoners' dilemmas into opportunities for mutual co-operation.

One result that arises from our simple analysis is that, for communities, social cohesion is superfluous. Our randomly-matched pairs of people in a community, as defined above, have no need for the artifact of social-capital investment. Sure, it makes mutual co-operation more profitable, and hence, more likely. But with a little bit of social knowledge and a commonly-held social standard of behaviour, people in our community could start co-operating in their economic interactions even without signalling to each other first by investing in a little social capital.

According to the taxonomy developed here, then, much of the dense social network in rural towns or urban neighbourhoods is really something more multidimensional. It is appropriate to study the network of social relationships under the heading of social cohesion, but it is important to recognize that these sometimes fondly described and folkloric relationships are, under certain conditions, sufficient to generate co-operative behaviour, but not necessary.

Social capital, in our simple set-up, allows the players of a single-encounter or one-shot prisoners' dilemma to avoid the pitfall of mutual defection. It is an individual investment that pays a return, whether monetary or purely psychological, to the person who makes the investment. Social cohesion is a characteristic of the economic environment in which these players are situated; past social-capital investments increase the degree of social cohesion today, and therefore the likelihood that co-operative behaviour will prevail today and in the future. Community obtains when people have more information about each other, and can follow a social standard of behaviour that enforces co-operative behaviour. In a sense, community favours social cohesion, but also renders it superfluous.

Trust

The original formula for knitted warmth given in Chapter 1 was Robert Putnam's definition of social capital: norms, networks, and trust. All of these are phenomena that are fundamentally characteristics of a group of people, not of individuals in isolation. They are "irreducibly social," in the words of McGill University philosopher Charles Taylor. Nevertheless, the economic approach, based on the starting point of the individual, has proved useful in interpreting them. This chapter has explored social capital, social cohesion, and community. How are these things related to norms, networks and trust? Norms, it has been argued, are characteristics of community, and economically productive co-operation can emerge even in their absence. Networks are generic opportunities for social capital. To make a social-capital investment, there must exist places to invest: neighbourhood groups, volunteer organizations, employer-sponsored seminars, meetings of the fishing community. Then where does trust come from? It emerges from the interaction of people in civil society: it is the expectation that, based on observing that your counterpart has invested in social capital, he will not defect when it comes time to play the prisoners' dilemma. Some — notably Fukuyama and Knack and Keefer — argue that social trust or generalized trust is what leads people to form organizations, so that associational life is the *outcome*. Trust is the cause and networks are the effect. Others posit the reverse: that a rich associational life generates trust. Sociologist Mark Granovetter's now-classic theory of trust supports this interpretation: "... social relations, rather than institutionalized arrangements or generalized morality are mainly responsible for the production of trust in economic life" (1985, pp. 490–91). Networks cause trust.

Microeconomic Evidence

Chapter 2 surveyed macroeconomic evidence of the economic consequences of social cohesion, evidence based on the comparison of countries. A growing body of microeconomic evidence supports the contention that social cohesion is good for the economy at the local level, too. In this vein, Ostrom's (1990) study of local regulatory institutions for the commons — inshore fisheries, community forests, farmer-managed irrigation systems — demonstrates that local community management can be more efficient than formal governmental regulation of the commons, and more efficient than establishing a private market in the natural resource. The locally-crafted rules and institutions that govern the use of the natural resource constitute an important example of community (according to the definition used in this chapter).

World Bank economists Deepa Narayan and Lant Pritchett (1999) studied a large number of Tanzanian villages. They, like Putnam in his study of Italy, compute an index of associational activity, and find that more such activity in a village is associated with appreciably higher per capita income. University of British Columbia economist John Helliwell (1996a) analyzed trust and associational activity (again using World Values Survey data) in the US and Canada. He found no evidence that faster growth occurred in higher-trust regions of those countries. Nevertheless, his analysis raised the possibility that regional differences in trust might influence patterns of migration. When people move within Canada or within the US, they do so overwhelmingly in response to the possibility of higher incomes. But perceived differences in trust appear to have an effect on migrants' decision making in addition to differences in income levels. Helliwell poses an interesting question in this connection: do migrants bring social capital with them, or do they adapt to the social capital patterns of their new region? The simple model introduced in this chapter would suggest the latter: people move to higher-trust regions and they become more trusting. Of course, a more complicated model would have to account for the effects of immigration. One would expect that in a population of people experiencing an influx of newcomers there would be some uncertainty about whether to trust any given individual. After all, that person might be a newcomer unaware of the local level of social cohesion.

The argument made at the beginning of this chapter is that social cohesion might make markets (or production processes) work better. Production teams are more likely to adopt more productive techniques, which might require intensive co-ordination. People will have better channels of information about economic opportunities. Buyers and sellers will be more willing to trust one another. In contrast, the emphasis from studies of poor economies — like the studies of Tanzanian villages or users of common-property resources mentioned above — is that social cohesion facilitates responses to the absence of markets. Mutual-insurance networks, local governance for the commons, and rotating savings and credit associations are substitutes for markets (for insurance, credit, or the use of natural resources) that fail to exist for various reasons. While these differing views appear inconsistent — is social cohesion a complement to, or substitute for, markets? — they can be at least partly reconciled by referring explicitly to the level of development of an economy. In the context of missing markets, social cohesion is a substitute; where the missing-market problem is not so pervasive (and indeed, even where it is), social cohesion can make market function more smoothly. (On the other hand, some types of markets may be inimical to social capital. Seabright (1997), for example, argues that privatizing the commons can destroy trust in the resource-using community. Pre-existing relations of co-operation might be weakened by the enforcement of private-property rights (a necessary pre-condition for markets), in part because the tradeability of property rights undermines reliable long-term relationships among the users of the resource.)

Summary: Microeconomic Logic and Social Cohesion

In summary, this chapter has introduced three basic microeconomic models. The first is the prisoners' dilemma, which shows that in settings where there is a nice outcome and a nasty outcome, sensible people might opt for the nasty outcome. Choosing the nice outcome typically involves some kind of co-operative behaviour. The unfortunate logic of the prisoners' dilemma describes many economic phenomena, and suggests that prosperous societies might be those that successfully resolve problems of this kind. The second model, the "social-capital" model, shows that investments in relationships and networks — social capital — can change the payoffs in the prisoners' dilemma. This might lead sensible people to choose the nice rather than the nasty outcome — to co-operate. A society's history of co-operative behaviour influences the future prospects for co-operation; this history, in a sense, is "social cohesion." The third model of this chapter is the "social standard of behaviour." This model illustrates that some societies might witness high levels of co-operation in situations like the prisoners' dilemma even *without* changing the payoffs. This can occur if people are embedded in a more complicated game where one person decides whether to co-operate today based on the level of co-operation she has observed in the past; if a society is fortunate to have a standard of behaviour to which many people subscribe, then co-operation might be an enduring phenomenon. Such a standard of behaviour is an alternative mechanism of social cohesion, an irreducibly social asset that makes society more prosperous.

Bibliographic Notes

Prime Minister Chrétien's views on communism and capitalism were made in Parliament on 22 February 2000, and reported, for example by Fife (2000). The difficulties of contracting in the relationship between manager and worker has a long history in economics, but has been most exhaustively analyzed over the years by Oliver Williamson; the most salient statement of the problem as applied to the workplace is Williamson, Wachter, and Harris (1975). The well-known "butcher-and-baker" citation of Adam Smith is from the *Wealth of Nations* (1776), Part I, Chap. II. The longer passage is taken from the *Theory of Moral Sentiments* (1759), Part III, Chap. V; I am grateful to my colleagues Mel Cross and Lars Osberg for pointing out this reference. That a general revision of mainstream economic thinking is underway, supporting my case in this chapter and in this book generally, is argued with more technical sophistication by Bowles and Gintis (2000). Much of the argument made in the section on co-operation and social cohesion is made in a more conventional (read: "mathematical") economic fashion in Dayton-Johnson (2001). The Canadian government definitions of social cohesion are cited in PRI (1999) and also SSCSAST (1999). The "social standard of behaviour" is developed in the context of economic theory by Okuno-Fujiwara and Postlewaite (1995); an excellent applied example is Ostrom's (1990) study of informal institutions for governing the commons. The contagion social standard of behaviour is analyzed by Kandori (1992).

4

Social Cohesion and Human Development

Every summer for the past several years, the United Nations Development Programme (UNDP) has released its annual Human Development Report on the state of economic and social progress around the world. The most visible element of the UNDP annual report is its Human Development Index (HDI), a statistic computed for every country, meant to measure the well-being of its citizens. In the international ranking of HDI levels, Canada has topped the list for many years running; the Liberal Party has routinely drawn much attention to this, while the Progressive-Conservative government in Ontario has used the ranking as a selling point to attract international businesses to the province.

Economists have typically used average income as a measure of well-being. If a country's average income rises over time (that is, if it enjoys sustained economic growth), people in that country can presumably use that income to purchase higher levels of health care and education; better health and educational outcomes, in turn, allow people to lead happier lives and participate more fully in national affairs. But if we really care about health and education, and income is just a means to pursuing those ends, why not simply measure health and education outcomes? Why the insistence on income? As a response to this critique, the UNDP computes the HDI as a weighted average of three components: average income (using the purchasing-power-parity technique discussed in Chapter 2); population health (measured by average life span); and education (measured by adult literacy rates and enrolment ratios). (A separate critique of the use of average income finds fault not in the use of income per se, but in the use of an average: the US has a higher average income than Canada, but also more inequality in the distribution of that income. Would people sacrifice some income in order to reduce inequality? If so, it is not clear that the average American is "better

Figure 4.1: HDI and Average Income Levels

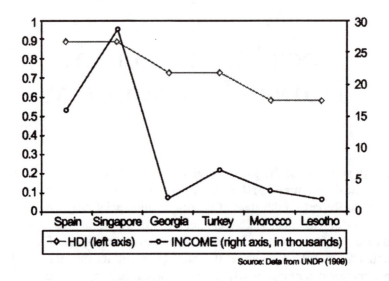

Source: Data from UNDP (1999)

off" than the average Canadian. The problem of inequality and its relationship to social cohesion is the subject of Chapter 5.)

Indeed, there are interesting divergences between average income and human development. Figure 4.1 shows average income levels and HDIs for six countries. There are three pairs of countries, each pair with virtually identical HDIs, but widely divergent average income levels. Singapore's average income is nearly twice that of Spain's but both have the same HDI; Turkey's average income is more than three times that of Georgia (the former Soviet republic, not the American state), but that extra income has not appreciably raised Turkish human development above the Georgian level. Lesotho, finally, with just over half of the average income of Morocco, nevertheless has an equal HDI. In all of these cases, countries that are poorer in the sense of money income have managed to achieve levels of health and education on par with considerably richer countries. The basic lesson of the HDI is that countries, even very poor countries, have choices to make regarding social policies that contribute to people's well-being.

Dalhousie University economist Lars Osberg and Andrew Sharpe of the Ottawa-based Centre for the Study of Living Standards have systematically looked at the relationship between GDP per capita and more inclusive indices of economic well-being in a group of industrialized countries. Figures 4.2, 4.3, and 4.4 show the evolution since

Figure 4.2: Well-Being in Canada, 1980–1997

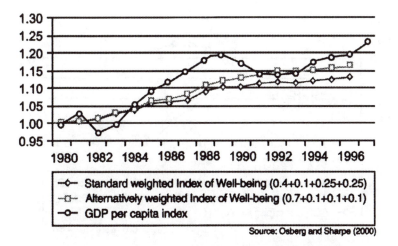

Source: Osberg and Sharpe (2000)

1980 of GDP per capita and two alternative measures of economic well-being in Canada, the United Kingdom, and the United States. Their indices of well-being have four components: (i) per capita consumption, an improvement on the less-precise measure of GDP per capita, and which is corrected for changes in life spans and leisure time; (ii) the accumulation of productive resources, including capital, housing, education, and research and development, adjusted for environmental costs and changes in foreign indebtedness; (iii) income distribution; and (iv) economic insecurity, based on the risk of unemployment, ill health, single-parent poverty, and poverty in old age. In shorthand terms, consumption, accumulation, distribution, and insecurity. (The two well-being indices shown in each of the figures differ in terms of the relative importance attributed to each of these four components, although each is based on the same four elements.)

For each case, the value of all indices is set at 1.0 in 1980. Thus, for Canada, for example, Figure 4.2 reveals that per capita GDP was about 23 percent higher in 1997 than it was in 1980. (This comparison accounts for inflation.) But by the first of the Osberg-Sharpe indices of well-being, Canadians were only about 13 percent "better off" at the latter date, accounting for accumulation, distribution, and insecurity. For the UK, the divergence between per capita income and well-being is even more stark. Per capita GDP was fully 40 percent higher in 1997 in the UK than in 1980. But the standard Osberg-Sharpe index of well-being, after plummeting to only 81 percent of its 1980 value in the early 1990s, was still only 91 percent of its 1980

Figure 4.3: Well-Being in the United Kingdom, 1980–1997

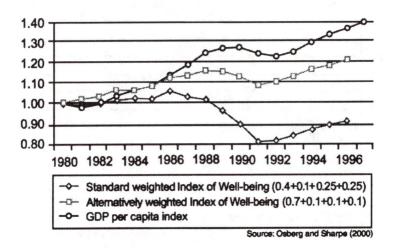

Figure 4.4: Well-Being in the United States, 1980–1997

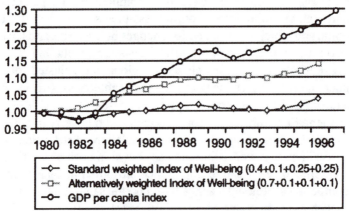

level at the end of the 1990s. The US experience lies somewhere between the Canadian and UK patterns: per capita income rose 30 percent over the eighties and nineties, but well-being was virtually unchanged, rising an anemic four percent. (In the Canadian, UK, and US cases, the "alternative" index of well-being shows a better performance than the standard index. The alternative index gives a greater weight to consumption growth than the standard index, and thus its fortunes more closely mirror those of per capita GDP.)

Osberg and Sharpe argue that if well-being is measured in ways not solely based on income levels, then the contribution of social cohesion will loom even larger. If indeed social cohesion enhances economic growth, it can be expected to raise consumption levels. At the same time, however, there is a close relationship between social cohesion and accumulation, distribution, and insecurity, the other components of the Osberg-Sharpe indices of well-being. Consider each in turn. Accumulation of physical capital might respond to higher levels of trust and denser networks for reasons detailed in Chapters 2 and 3. Accumulation of human capital — education — is discussed at greater length in this chapter. The relationship between education and social cohesion is a reciprocal one: appropriate educational policies can build social cohesion; it is also true that more educated people tend to have higher levels of trust and associational activity. The relationship between inequality and social cohesion is the subject of Chapter 5, and this relationship is also likely reciprocal: high inequality erodes social cohesion, while social cohesion might increase support for egalitarian policies that reduce inequalities. Finally, social relationships underlying cohesion can reduce economic insecurities based on illness and poverty, whether through public policy or through private responses. This, indeed, is the common theme of the health-related research reviewed in the first part of this chapter.

The preceding chapters can be seen as an elaborate attempt to persuade the reader that social cohesion can contribute to economic growth. By enhancing the prospects for co-operative behaviour, social cohesion will raise growth rates and therefore lead to higher average income levels. But perhaps we should take our cue from the UNDP and acknowledge that income is a sloppy signal of material well-being; accordingly, this chapter explores the impact of social cohesion on other components of human development: namely, health and education.

Although health and education are most important precisely because of their direct effect on people's well-being, a book on the economics of social cohesion would be remiss if it did not remind its readers that these goods produce substantial economic benefits as well. A healthy and well-educated population is more productive in the broadest sense of the word. Thus if social cohesion affects a society's health and education, this affects well-being both directly and indirectly via its effect on economic performance.

Health

That social cohesion might prove beneficial for people's health is a longer-running and perhaps better founded contention than the link between social cohesion and the economy. That stems largely from the widely disseminated research of UK health scientist Richard Wilkinson. Wilkinson discovered a strong relationship between income inequality in a jurisdiction and indicators of health — principally death rates. Where inequality is greater, death rates are higher. As Wilkinson wrote in 1995:

> [A]t least eight different research workers or groups have reported statistically significant relations between income distribution and measures of mortality using 10 separate sets of data. Of these eight, one has used data exclusively on developing countries, two on a mixture of developed and developing countries, and five exclusively on developed countries. The association has been found to be independent of fertility, maternal literacy, and education in developing countries and of average incomes, absolute levels of poverty, smoking, racial differences, and various measures of the provision of medical services in developed countries.

Like the macroeconomic evidence on social cohesion and growth presented in Chapter 2, Wilkinson is making a claim about the relationships among several variables at once. To put the matter differently, one might expect that inequality and death rates would be positively related, without necessarily claiming that inequality itself causes higher death rates. For example, where there is greater inequality, it means that there is relatively more poverty; after all, the more unequal the distribution of income, the greater the proportion of people at the poor end of the spectrum. It could be, then, that poverty itself pushes death rates higher as the poor are less able to secure the goods and services they need to sustain their livelihoods. Or, it may not be poverty that causes higher mortality: perhaps the poor are more likely to engage in risky behaviour like smoking. Or, given that inequality is higher in the poorer countries of Latin America than in the relatively richer countries of North America and Europe, perhaps it is just the lower average incomes of Latin America that cause mortality rates to be higher there than in the richer but more equal countries of the northern hemisphere. For any of these reasons, income inequality and mortality rates would be strongly correlated, even though income inequality is not the cause of the higher death rates.

What Wilkinson has uncovered is based on multi-variable analysis: inequality appears to cause poorer health outcomes for society, even accounting for differences in poverty rates, for differences in absolute income levels among societies, for differences in the number of smokers, and all the other factors cited above by Wilkinson. The interpretation of this research, then, is that if one compared two societies identical in every respect (average income, rates of smoking, even levels of absolute poverty) except that one had greater income inequality, then death rates would be higher in the more unequal society. Something about inequality appears to cause greater mortality.

Consider research from the US (Kawachi and Kennedy, 1999). At higher levels of household income, fewer and fewer survey respondents report only fair or poor health, which is precisely what we would expect. However, this trend differs for two types of societies: high-inequality and low-inequality states of the US. The trend is always downward, but for any given household income level, the average health of a person is likely to be worse in a state with higher levels of inequality that in a more equal state. If this holds among states in the US, it is plausible that it holds also among countries, as Wilkinson has claimed.

This is mostly about income inequality. Trying to explain phenomena like these, however, tends to quickly lead to a discussion of social cohesion. The general formulation is that income inequality weakens social cohesion, which has a direct impact on health. (Chapter 5 will look much more closely at income inequality itself.) Is it social cohesion directly that, independently of the health-care system, smoking behaviour, income levels, and so many other factors, contributes to good health?

Two widely-known US studies demonstrated to doctors that social cohesion has a health payoff. The first is a long-term case study of the town of Roseto, Pennsylvania in the 1960s and a neighbouring town with similar rates of smoking, obesity, and diets. The chief difference between the two towns was that there were twice as many civic organizations per capita and, probably not coincidentally, more cohesive community relationships in Roseto; Roseto's rate of death from heart disease was half that of the other town. Over time, Roseto's level of social cohesion, the density of civic organizations that reflected past social-capital investments, began to depreciate, and the death rate from heart disease rose concomitantly.

A contemporary study of Alameda County, California, directly measured the social relationships of people. Those with more linkages to others through family, marriage, friendships, church, and civic organizations faced lower risk of death at any point in time. That is, after the original survey, those without such social links were two to three times more likely to die during the subsequent nine years. Social relationships, social supports, social connectedness — individual investments in what we have called social capital — save lives. And, to use the taxonomy developed in the last chapter, it is social cohesion, not just social capital, that saves lives: people invest in social relationships, but they only pay off if others do the same. It is not so mysterious that more linked communities and neighbourhoods would have lower rates of death and illness than otherwise identical communities. Extended families and neighbours look after one another and provide support that can help directly (like a ride to the hospital) or indirectly (by reducing stress).

Two principal interpretations have been put forward to explain the link between economic inequality and population health levels. The first is that proposed by Wilkinson, mentioned above. This approach has been dubbed the "psychosocial" link. The presence of economic inequality invites the less-fortunate to compare themselves to those better off; it is relative, not absolute, deprivation that leads to damaging health effects. While this logic is inspired in part by the Roseto and Alameda County studies, it emphasizes society-wide inequality rather than community-level characteristics per se. McMaster University health economists Lavis and Stoddart summarize the appeal of this approach in the following terms:

Psychological processes arising from perception of one's status, economic insecurity or relative deprivation are said to translate into important changes in the nervous, endocrine, and immune systems — changes which in turn lead to deteriorations in mental and physical health. This is not as unlikely as it may first sound. Consider, for example, the flu that often strikes students after their exams: stress can have a direct impact on the immune system. Now consider what lifelong exposure to constant and relatively high levels of daily stress associated with economic insecurity, relative deprivation, feelings of helplessness or lack of control over one's life might do!

The competing line of explanation is the so-called "neo-material" view; roughly speaking, this view holds that it is not inequality per se that damages population health, but that independent factors that create socioeconomic inequality also create poor population health. (In the words of Ross et al. (2000, p. 1202): "The neomaterial interpretation says that health inequalities result from the differential accumulation of exposures and experiences that have their sources in the material world.") Lynch and his co-authors point out in a 2000 study that income inequality widened drastically in Great Britain between the mid-1970s and the 1990s, but mortality rates for middle-age and older people declined drastically as well. A literal reading of the psychosocial pathway would have predicted the opposite.

It is interesting to point out that important evidence in favour of the neo-material interpretation stems from a recent comparative study of the relationship between inequality and population health in Canada and the US by Statistics Canada researchers and others (Ross et al., 2000). This research team found, as many researchers have, that mortality rates and inequalities are significantly lower in Canada than in the US. They furthermore found that among US metropolitan areas, and among states in the US, there is a significant relationship between local mortality rates (for various age groups) and local inequality (measured by the share of total income accruing to the poorest half of the local population). Nevertheless, this relationship is not significant for Canadian metropolitan areas or among Canadian provinces. Ross and her co-authors suggest (2000, p. 1202) that "[i]f income inequality is less linked to investments in health related public infrastructure, the aggregate level association between income inequality and health may break down." In broad brush strokes, access to health care is much more closely related to personal income in the US than it is in Canada, so that the negative impacts of inequality are more notoriously reflected in health outcomes in the US. It may also be that the relationship between inequality and poor population health is weak at relatively lower levels of inequality — like those observed in Canada — but if inequality were to increase here, negative health consequences would be observed here as in the US.

It is important to emphasize the respects in which the psychosocial and neo-material pathways are similar. Both predict that income inequality has deleterious effects, and both suggest that policies to decrease inequality, should, all else being equal, improve population health. It is also important to point out that inequality has been increasing in Canada during the last ten years (a trend that will be further analyzed in the following chapter), and that mechanisms to equalize the delivery of health care across the country have weakened over the same period. The comparative US-Canada study by Statistics Canada does not rule out the possibility of harmful effects of inequality on population health in this country in the future.

Schools

I recently talked with a friend from Spain who is now an economics professor in the US. He characterized a principal difference between Spain and North America as follows: when two strangers in their thirties meet in Spain, they presume that they are fundamentally alike. When two such strangers meet in North America their initial presumption is that they are fundamentally dissimilar. In each case, communication might change the strangers' opinion, but the initial expectation is different in the two settings. He attributed the Spanish attitude in large measure to shared experiences of upbringing that simply do not exist in North America, and that largely do not exist in Spain today. Two 35-year-old Spanish strangers will know the colour of the cover of the textbook they both used, in different cities, at the same age. In addition, both will have grown up watching the same limited number of state-run television networks and listening to the same limited number of state-run radio networks. This has engendered a strong sense of fellow feeling, one that the evidence of previous chapters suggests will lead to higher levels of trust and co-operation.

It must be recalled, of course, that this shared educational background occurred against the backdrop, and in large measure because of, the Franco dictatorship. My Spanish friend, and many readers of this book, would largely applaud the fact that schoolchildren in democratic Spain are now educated in Galician and Catalan and other regional languages. But we might also lament the loss of shared experiences, independent of their origins in the policies of a dictatorship.

Does education itself contribute to social capital accumulation? That is, are more educated people more likely to join groups and volunteer? Are they more trusting of their fellow nationals and of others generally? The evidence on this is surprisingly weak. Table 4.1 reports the correlation between years of education and the number of group types to which people belong and for which they volunteer. For each of the G-7 countries, the table computes the correlation between a person's level of education (measured by her school-leaving age) and various measures of that person's social

Table 4.1: Correlation between Levels of Education and Social Cohesion

Correlation of a person's years of education with ...

	... groups to which she belongs	... groups for which she performs unpaid work	... level of trust in her fellow nationals
France	0.22632	0.16034	-0.10384
Great Britain	0.31748	0.17860	-0.07451
West Germany	0.17640	0.12604	-0.13231
Italy	0.28181	0.15529	-0.07962
USA	0.29997	0.19082	0.03592
Canada	0.20641	0.08722	-0.09989
Japan	0.04714	0.02364	0.00461

Source: Computed from WVS (1999).

capital or social cohesion. The first two measures of social capital are the number of group types to which the person belongs and for which she volunteers, respectively. The third is her expressed level of trust in her fellow French people, Britons, etc. If the correlation is positive and perfect — if survey respondents with the most education also belong to the most groups, for example, then the correlation coefficient would be equal to one. (Likewise, if the correlation is negative and perfect, the correlation coefficient would be negative one. In that case, those with the lowest levels of education would always belong to the largest number of groups.)

The correlation between years of education and associational activity is positive and generally significant in all of the countries considered. (The general exception is Japan.) More educated people are more likely to be members of more types of groups, and to perform volunteer work for more types of groups. In general, the correlation is higher between educational levels and memberships than between education and voluntary activity. Nevertheless, the magnitude of the effect of education is smaller than one might at first suspect. Perhaps even more surprising is that more years of education is correlated with lower levels of trust in one's compatriots in many countries. (Moreover, the correlations between education and trust in many cases are not significant.) What this suggests is that a gross increase in education does not necessarily make a person more trusting of her compatriots; it may be associated with more group activity, but the effect is not huge.

But this does not contradict our Spanish example. There, it is essentially the shared experience of a common educational content and style that provided fellow feeling and trust. That is a different proposition than merely saying that more education is associated with more trust and more associational activity for any given individual. What is important is that everyone has more or less the same education. Indeed, to the extent that the survey data used in Table 4.1 can say anything on this score, perhaps one should look at the correlation between inequalities in educational attainment and national levels of trust or associational activity. For example, the standard deviation of educational levels in the US is 2.3 years, while in Italy, it is 3.6 years. This means that the average variation in schooling levels is higher among people in Italy than it is in the US. For the countries in Table 4.1, the correlation between this measure of variation in school-leaving age and the average level of trust in one's compatriots is -0.72. (In part because of the small number of countries being considered, the correlation is not statistically significant.) Countries where the schooling experience of different individuals is more varied — as indicated by the time each person spends in school — also happen to have lower levels of trust among nationals. The correlation between the standard deviation in years of schooling and group memberships is -0.78; between the variation in schooling and voluntary activity, it is -0.59. It should be borne in mind that these statements are being made for a small number of observations, and that these strong negative correlations might disappear if more countries were considered at once. Moreover, as is always the case, two-way correlations should not be confused with causation: it could very well be that some third factor, or a whole set of other factors, is driving the association between variation in schooling and trust. It should also be borne in mind that we are merely considering one dimension along which the experience of schooling is "shared": its length. This is an admittedly crude indicator. With information on other aspects of the schooling experience in these countries, one could form a more complete picture of the relationship between shared schooling experience and fellow feeling in a country.

In a 2000 paper, economists Mark Gradstein and Moshe Justman formulated an interesting model of publicly-provided schooling as a social-cohesion delivery mechanism. In their model, public schooling that instils shared norms and values provides three benefits. First, it reduces the cost of economic production and exchange if it can instil norms against opportunism and in favour of co-operative behaviour. This is different than the mechanisms outlined in the previous chapter. There, people invested in social capital and in doing so, changed the incentives they faced such that co-operation became, potentially, more attractive. Schooling, of course, can instil a preference for co-operation per se. Second, by providing shared experiences, schooling reduces "differences in language, custom, or religion [that] can give rise to misunderstandings that undermine the efficiency of production and exchange" (p. 880). Third, social cohesion reduces the basis for unproductive conflict based on ethnic or cultural group identities. Such conflicts include not only the extreme of civil war, but conflicts over government spending policies that can cripple economic performance. The downside of social cohesion in the Gradstein/Justman model is that the new values instilled into children may differ from those of the parents and the link between parent and child is weakened. Parents, in this model, decide whether to invest in public or private schooling for their children. They may face a trade-off between the strength of their cultural link to their children, and the social cohesion benefits of universally similar schooling.

The model focuses on wasteful lobbying and inter-group wrangling among competing ethnic groups as a drag on economic growth. (This is what economists call "rent-seeking behaviour.") Among the results of the model, there will be greater investment in schooling and higher income levels in the future if public schooling is imposed, in comparison to a world in which parents send their kids to private schools. The higher level of social cohesion made possible by a universal schooling experience raises the return to human-capital investments. That is, not only does public schooling contribute to social cohesion, but the higher level of social cohesion makes education more attractive.

An interesting aspect of the Gradstein/Justman model, and of the consideration of schooling as a mechanism for constructing social cohesion more generally, is that it provides a justification for public provision, not merely public financing, of education. That is, there are well-rehearsed arguments for universal education, but those would be completely compatible with competitive private schools and vouchers provided by government to all parents. Why is it that governments not only pay for education, but they also provide it? The answer may be that such universally provided schooling much more efficiently instils shared norms and values.

There is also some fuzziness regarding the line between human and social capital provided by schooling. Human capital, as it has been conventionally conceived in the social sciences, is like a lathe or a hammer: it's useful, it's yours, and it will increase your lifetime stream of earnings relative to those who have less of it. Certain technical skills provided by schooling clearly fit this mold. To the extent that schools impart norms favouring co-operation, this can be considered social capital accumulation. A child who has such norms, in isolation, is not likely to have higher earnings than one who does not. Of course, a society where such a norm is widespread might have higher average earnings than one which does not — but that's something quite different than having more lathes. Social capital provided by schooling is economically productive, roughly speaking, only if it is shared. This, indeed, is the crux of the definition of social capital developed in the previous chapter. But many of the most fundamental human-capital skills provided by schooling, most notably literacy and numeracy, blur the distinction between human and social capital. Literacy and numeracy are economically productive in large measure because they reduce the costs of co-ordinating activities in markets and firms. Is this social or human capital? Further research could be devoted to this question, but the important point at this juncture is that publicly-provided schooling might be uniquely capable of investing in these critical forms of non-physical capital.

Conclusion

Social cohesion contributes to narrow measures of economic prosperity: levels and growth rates of average income. Social cohesion likewise contributes to broader-based measures of material well-being, such as the United Nations Development Programme's Human Development Index, which accounts for income, but also for achievements in health and education. In this chapter we have seen that economic inequality is damaging to population health. The exact link between the two concepts is still in dispute, but many researchers agree that the fraying of social cohesion under conditions of inequality contributes to disappointing society-wide health outcomes. There is furthermore good reason to suspect that the educational success of a country is linked to social cohesion: more cohesive societies can be expected to invest more in education, while shared experiences of schooling can contribute to the sense of fellow feeling that promotes economic success.

Bibliographic Notes

The UNDP Human Development Reports are published annually by Oxford University Press. The specific country comparisons made in this chapter are drawn from the 1999 report, p. 129. Srinivasan (1994) provides a rare but reasonable critique of the HDI from the economic perspective. Probably the most important criticism made by Srinivasan is that, despite the interesting comparisons between countries like Turkey and Georgia discussed above, the HDI and average income are very highly correlated overall: countries with high HDIs have high average income levels, and countries with low HDIs have low average income levels. Given this, Srinivasan argues that the contribution of the HDI to our understanding of well-being is minimal. On this, see also the scatter plots in Chapter 2 of Ray (1998). The Osberg-Sharpe indices of economic well-being, and their relationship to social capital, are developed in Osberg and Sharpe (2000). They extend the analysis reviewed in this chapter for Canada, the UK, and the US, to other OECD (Organization for Economic Co-operation and Development) countries. The Roseto and Alameda County studies of social relationships and health are summarized, with all the appropriate citations, in Lavis and Stoddart (2000). Townson (1999) is a useful review of the psychosocial approach in the Canadian context. Lynch et al. (2000), strong advocates of the neo-material interpretation of the health effects of inequality, compare their preferred explanation to the psychosocial interpretation and find that "a combination of the individual income and neo-material interpretations is a better fit to the available evidence on income inequality and health, is more comprehensive, and has greater potential to inform interventions that advance public health and reduce inequalities." Muntaner and Lynch (1999) critique the psychosocial explanation from the standpoint of sociological theory. Raphael (2000) provides a useful summary of views of the relationship between inequality and health at the federal, provincial, and local levels in Canada over time. He concludes that while recognition of the link between inequality and population health is widespread among policy-makers, little policy reflects that awareness.

5

Inequality

My friend and colleague Lars Osberg, among Canada's leading analysts of social policy, addressed a Senate committee looking into the
issue of social cohesion in October 1998. His message: "There really
does seem to be some economic payoff to something that we would
call social cohesion or equality." His statement raises a number of
issues. First, there are positive economic consequences to social
cohesion, just as we saw in Chapter 2. Second, Professor Osberg
explicitly equates social cohesion and economic equality. Certainly
concern for the fraying of Canada's social fabric is closely related to
worries about the widening of the distribution of income. John
Myles, at the time a visiting researcher at Statistics Canada, told the
same Senate committee that "If rising inequality in the distribution
of income has a tendency to weaken the sense of reciprocity and
increase the sense of distance between 'us' and 'them', Canadians
have something to worry about."

Before exploring the link between economic equality and social
cohesion, it is worth looking at the extent to which income inequality
is widening in Canada and elsewhere. Figure 5.1 plots the evolution
of the *Gini coefficient* for six countries, including Canada, during the
period 1969–1997. The Gini coefficient is a commonly-used measure
of inequality. Roughly speaking, it is computed by adding up all the
differences in income between every pair of income-earners in an
economy; that difference is then divided by the size of the population.
Thus, the more unequally distributed is income in an economy, the
larger the Gini coefficient, which in theory can range from zero
(perfect equality) to one (complete inequality). To give a context for
the numbers in Figure 5.1, Gini coefficients in many Eastern European countries before the fall of the Berlin Wall were in the neighbourhood of 0.25, while in many Latin American countries (e.g.,
Brazil, Colombia, Guatemala) the value hovers around 0.6. The figures used to plot Figure 5.1 are based on *disposable* income, income
after subtracting taxes and adding in transfer payments from the

Figure 5.1: Trends in the Gini Coefficient of Inequality

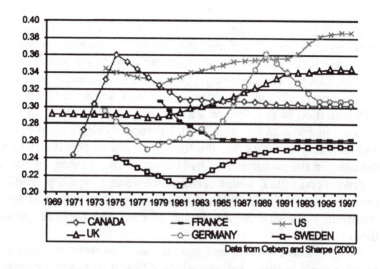

Data from Osberg and Sharpe (2000)

government. Gini coefficients computed on the basis of income before taxes and transfers could potentially be quite different.

The data show, most notably, marked increases in inequality beginning in the early 1980s in the US and UK. In the former case, the Gini coefficient rises from about 0.33 to 0.39 over that period; in the latter case, the rise is from about 0.29 to 0.34. In Canada, inequality rose during the early 1970s, and fell sharply in the late 1970s. The tendency since the early 1980s has been more or less flat, with a slight downward cast. Rising inequality, then, has not been a feature of all advanced economies during the last quarter century. In Canada's case, this conclusion likely relies critically on the equalizing effects of taxes and transfers on the distribution of income among Canadians. Nevertheless, the equalizing effects of government finances were not sufficient to stem rising inequality in the US, UK, and Sweden. In all countries, inequality is likely to be an increasingly important policy concern given varying degrees of opposition to the taxes and transfers that tend to reduce it.

Are social cohesion and economic equality conceptually distinct? Historically, the two things are quite different. Equality as a political rallying cry arose, of course, most notably during the French Revolution; pre-revolutionary French society exhibited considerable economic heterogeneity but a certain degree of social cohesion.

Historian Roland Mousnier has recounted, in amazing detail, the cultural rationale attributed to the stark social hierarchy of the *ancien régime*. Indeed, development economists Jean-Marie Baland and Jean-Philippe Platteau distinguish between economic homogeneity (equality in incomes) and cultural homogeneity (shared adherence to a single set of values). Rural communities in poor countries might exhibit, like pre-revolutionary France, large differences in income levels among people, but have a common acceptance that such differentiation is appropriate and proper. And indeed, in agrarian villages in India today or in feudal France, values shared by rich and poor might dictate that the former have a responsibility to aid the latter in the occurrence of bad harvests. These examples suffice to drive a conceptual wedge between economic inequality, based on the variation in livelihoods among a group of people, and social cohesion, evidenced by the degree of trust and networks among those people.

While social cohesion and equality are two different things, in practice their fortunes are nevertheless linked in modern capitalist societies. There are many reasons to suspect that a cohesive society will have relatively lower levels of inequality, and that economies with more equal distribution of wealth and income will have higher levels of social cohesion. Furthermore, both low levels of social cohesion and high levels of inequality can be bad for economic performance.

But the distinction is important. Social cohesion and inequality affect growth through different channels. Social cohesion tempers the nature of our interactions with others, including others with whom we work and exchange. A fraying of social cohesion can hamper economic performance through its effect on the quality of those personal and impersonal interactions. Chapter 3 in particular attempts to put some flesh on this argument. These effects can take many forms. Workplaces and markets are less efficient than they would be with more social cohesion. Alternatively, polarized groups engage in wasteful lobbying that reduces the efficiency of fiscal policy. Or those groups engage in more destructive social conflict that brings economic activity to a standstill.

Inequality in incomes and wealth, however, affects growth primarily by denying opportunities to the poor. Most notably in advanced economies like Canada's, inequality can deprive the poor of opportunities to invest in a level of education that would be socially optimal. Many economists also argue that the poor are unable to borrow funds in order to invest them, not only in education, but in other productive enterprises. The overall rate of investment and innovation in unequal societies is thus lower and less efficient than would be the case if the poor had better access to the levers of economic growth.

To the extent that distinct groups in society are defined by economic class, frayed social cohesion and inequality overlap considerably. Then, conflict arising from low social cohesion is largely caused by economic inequality. But I would argue that inter-group competition of this sort is a different kind of damper on growth than the confining constraints on economic decision-making imposed on the poor.

Economists did not always think this way. Textbooks and policy advisors once routinely lamented the "equity/efficiency trade-off." Some still do. This trade-off thinking proposes that equality can be pursued by a society only at the cost of forgone growth, and that growth comes by sacrificing equality. There are many dimensions to this idea. First is the hypothesis that economic growth, at least for a time, generates inequality. Owners of capital and workers in firms in more dynamic sectors will have disproportionately larger earnings than those in less dynamic parts of the economy. This will tend to make the distribution of earnings more unequal. If you want the efficient expansion of new leading sectors, in this view, you will have to accept increasing income disparities. Another version of the trade-off is that efforts by policy-makers to redress economic inequality come at the expense of efficiency. Arthur Okun, who was an economic advisor to US president Lyndon Johnson, popularized the notion that redistributive taxation could only be carried out with a "leaky bucket." Transferring resources from richer to poorer people would tend to dribble some of those resources on the ground along the way. High marginal tax rates, proponents of this view argue, distort the incentives of wealthy people to work and invest, thus depressing economic growth. This negative effect, furthermore, outweighs any benefits derived from the improved economic prospects of the poor beneficiaries of redistributive largesse.

Inequality and Growth: Evidence

One can imagine economists' surprise, then, when a host of carefully conceived macroeconomic studies demonstrated a robust and decidedly negative relationship between measures of inequality and economic growth. Two 1994 papers show that, if one carefully compares a group of economies at a point in time, those with greater economic equality will grow faster from that point onward.

The first, by Torsten Persson and Guido Tabellini of Stockholm University and Università di Brescia, respectively, uses historical data on nine of today's industrialized countries. They split the data into twenty-year intervals, which has the effect of multiplying the number of observations and the precision with which various effects can be measured. Their measure of inequality is the share of pre-tax income of the top 20 percent of income earners in a country. The higher this share, the more unequal the distribution of income. In the Persson/Tabellini data set, this income share ranged from a low of 38 percent (for Sweden in the 1970s) to a high of 67 percent (for Finland in the 1930s). Thus, for example, the richest fifth of Finns in the 1930s earned fully two-thirds of pre-tax income in Finland. Their measure of economic performance is growth of per capita GDP. They interpret the measure of inequality at the *start* of each time interval as a determinant of subsequent average-income growth. This way they are able to rule out, at least partially, that the causation might run in the opposite direction. (Thus, observed rates of income growth from 1930 to 1950, say, do not affect the level of inequality in 1930.) Persson and Tabellini employ the multivariate regression framework discussed at length in Chapter 2 (with regard to the Barro and Knack/Keefer research). In a variety of alternative models, they find a consistently negative and significant effect of the size of the income share accruing to the richest fifth of a country on growth of average income. In short, controlling for a wide range of other factors, the more unequally distributed is income at one point in time, the slower will be growth over the next few decades.

Alberto Alesina and Dani Rodrik, both Harvard University economists, analyze inequality and growth in a 1994 paper complementary to the Persson/Tabellini work. Alesina and Rodrik use a data set from a cross section of 50 to 70 countries (depending on the particular statistical model) for the period 1960–1985. As a measure of inequality, they use the Gini coefficient for each country. Recall that the Gini coefficient is the measure of inequality depicted in Figure 5.1. They compute the Gini coefficient of income inequality and land-holding inequality for each country in 1960. (Land-holding inequality is an imperfect measure of disparities in wealth, rather than income.) They too find a significant negative effect of inequality in 1960 on growth over the subsequent 25 years.

Inequality and Growth: Explanations

How could generations of economists have gotten the story wrong?
The conventional wisdom quite clearly held that equality was not
good for growth; conversely, inequality should at least not be *bad*
for growth. What are the overlooked mechanisms running from inequality to growth? The two studies reviewed above suggest similar
explanations. Both Alesina/Rodrik and Persson/Tabellini hypothe-
size that inequality in a country increases the pressure for redistributive public finance — higher tax rates for the wealthy and transfers
to the poor. Both studies essentially provide theoretical models of
economies in which people vote on tax rates for the wealthy. (In
practice, this could refer to corporate taxes or personal income taxes
on above-average earners.) The greater the inequality, the higher the
democratically-chosen tax rate on richer citizens; after all, there's a
greater constituency for high taxes in an unequal society. Poorer
citizens stand to benefit from government transfers in particular,
which can be financed from taxes on the wealthy. This is a case
where intergroup *electoral* conflict aligns perfectly along economic
class lines. Inequality and the lack of social cohesion are one and the
same thing.

Higher taxes for the wealthy, in turn, depress incentives for the
wealthy to invest; and investment, of course, is the motor of economic growth. For the wealthy person considering investing in a new
business or expanding an existing one, a higher tax on his return from
that investment will, all else being equal, reduce the magnitude of
the desired investment. In terms of economic theory, investors will
install new capital up to the point where the cost of the last unit of
capital installed is just equal to the benefit it provides. An increase
in the rate of taxation reduces the benefit of the last unit installed,
while leaving the cost of capital unchanged. The rational adjustment
for the investor is to scale back investment. There is no dispute that
lower rates of investment in new capital will reduce economic
growth in turn.

The astute reader may have noticed that this explanation of the
statistical evidence linking inequality and slow growth, which is
plausible enough on logical grounds, actually confirms the conventional "leaky-bucket" wisdom. It is precisely *because* the redistributive policies of the welfare state are inefficient (for the promotion of
growth) that inequality is bad for growth. More unequal countries
face political pressures to redistribute income with its attendant

dampening effect on growth. This is bad news for policy-makers, however. If inequality is bad for growth, the obvious policy recommendation is to reduce inequality. But the basic means of reducing inequality is redistributive income transfers from the rich to the poor. And that, in this view, slows growth. The conundrum is a sort of Catch-22. Economies with unequally-distributed income are more or less stuck.

The redistributive-pressure hypothesis is not the only explanation of the evidence linking low growth and inequality. First of all, there are problems with the applicability of the model's logic. It relies, plausibly enough, on a well-functioning democratic system. If the average income of voters is different — in particular, if it is higher — than the average income of people generally, then there is no guarantee that voters will impose high rates of personal-income or corporate taxation. Moreover, in countries with tenuous representative democracy, there is little reason to suspect that governments will choose high rates of taxes on the wealthy. (They might, if they are afraid of violent dissent; but there are other, non-fiscal, means of quelling dissent.) Second, the conclusion is called into question by research looking directly at the link between the magnitude of transfer payments and growth rates. Transfer payments include social assistance, social insurance, and social security payments of all types; they are made possible by tax revenues. Thus, countries with higher rates of taxes on the wealthy will also likely have higher levels of transfer payments. A 1994 paper by Columbia University economist Roberto Perotti, again in a multivariate regression framework, estimates the effect of the magnitude of transfer payments on investment rates (the ratio of investment to GDP). In his statistical analysis, transfers contribute *positively* to the rate of investment: controlling for a host of other factors, countries with higher rates of transfer payments have higher investment rates. This flies more or less in the face of the redistributive-pressure argument.

A second class of explanations, which might be termed the "social-conflict" mechanisms, is similar to the redistributive-pressure hypothesis. In this view, inequality leads to social conflict — which can be measured in terms of successful and unsuccessful coups, people killed in political actions, and assassinations and other indicators of unrest — that depresses investors' confidence. Alesina and Perotti, in a 1996 paper, estimated regression models of political instability and investment behaviour. They found, not surprisingly, that, controlling for many factors, inequality leads to an increase in political instability, which leads in turn to a decrease in investment. What is perhaps surprising about their results is that they claim that the negative effect of inequality on investment is fully accounted for through its effect on social instability. That is, there is no residual effect of inequality on investment independent of inequality's effect on unrest. Their evidence is suggestive but not conclusive; alternative ways of analyzing the statistical data might yield different results. While their results are sufficiently robust to confidently state that social conflict depresses economic performance, there may well be a role for other mechanisms running from inequality to growth. Consequently, there is still reason to critically assess other avenues linking inequality and economic performance.

Yet a third class of models is frequently characterized as "imperfect asset markets" explanations. Asset markets are any markets in which borrowers secure funds to invest in capital — physical capital, such as machines and trucks, or human capital, such as education and training. Suppose that a poor person knows of a capital investment opportunity that would generate a return of 10 percent annually. That is, if she invests $1,000, the project will earn $100 in the first year. She must borrow the start-up capital; after all, she is poor. If the prevailing rate of interest charged by banks is 7 percent, this is a good investment, for her and for the bank that lends to her. In the first year, the bank would get $70, and our investor $30, after making her loan payment. Now suppose that the investor has no wealth she can post as collateral, and that the bank refuses to lend. That is a market imperfection: profitable exchange opportunities fail to come about. The consequence is that a large number of potential productive investments are not made every year, depressing growth. In developing countries, the number of people thus excluded from capital markets is a staggering proportion of the total population. If they could, many of those shut out from lending could begin or expand operations on family farms, in small-scale manufacturing, or retail activities. The forgone GDP is huge. In all countries, rich and poor, a concrete consequence of imperfect asset markets is that people invest too little in education and training. The most basic investment that could be increased among the poor worldwide is in human capital.

Notice a number of features of the imperfect-asset-markets explanation. First, it is consistent with Perotti's evidence regarding transfers. Any policy that transfers spending power to the poor will, in this view, improve investment directly, and growth indirectly.

Second, there is hope for policy-makers to attack the root causes of disappointing growth performance. Transfers to the poor are within the purview of the government, and, if properly designed, will not choke off growth. Third, this mechanism is quite distinct from social cohesion. It is inequality itself that causes the failure of growth, by restricting the opportunities of a large part of the population. The mechanism is also fundamentally an economic one: it operates by constraining the economic power of the poor. In contrast, the redistributive-pressure hypothesis is based on electoral conflict, with its roots in inequality, perhaps. The social-conflict hypothesis operates by social, rather than economic, means. Both of these latter mechanisms rely more on the fraying of social cohesion than on inequality per se.

How important is the imperfect-asset-markets mechanism in practice? While there is substantial evidence from countries around the world that asset markets of all kinds do not function perfectly, there is less evidence regarding the link between such market imperfections and investment and growth. More research has been done on the influence of transfers and social unrest on growth. This is because it is somewhat easier to measure transfers and unrest than the "degree of incompleteness" of asset markets. Nevertheless, Roland Bénabou of Princeton University points out that indirect evidence supports the imperfect-asset-markets hypothesis. He sees confirmation of the hypothesis by comparing the effect of redistributive transfers, notably public education spending, and government consumption (non-investment spending by the government on things like running bureaucracies). If credit markets constrain the opportunities of the poor, then public education functions as a transfer of resources to the poor that acts as a substitute for credit markets. Instead of borrowing money to finance their education, the poor (and all others) receive education for free from the government. In the presence of constraints, then, government spending on education should contribute positively to growth. Barro's celebrated growth study, reviewed in Chapter 2, and virtually any similar study before or since, has found that education (measured by expenditures or by enrolments) contributes massively to economic growth. As we saw earlier in this chapter, other transfers that "relax" the credit constraint facing the poor also promote investment and growth. Barro's study nevertheless found that other sorts of government spending had a significantly negative effect on growth. Now if there were no asset-market imperfections, all government spending should have a negative effect on growth. Such spending is paid for by tax revenues, and taxes on economic activity depress that activity. Government consumption indeed depresses growth, but redistributive transfers raise growth rates. The positive impact of giving opportunities to the poor appears to outweigh the negative effects of taxation. Bénabou interprets the statistical analysis regarding public education, transfers, and other government spending, as supportive of the imperfect-asset-markets story.

Inequality and Social Cohesion

If we take Bénabou's cue, then there is an important negative effect of inequality per se on economic growth in the world today, distinct from the effect of social cohesion. This is the effect of imperfect asset markets. But things are complicated. It might also be that inequality affects social cohesion itself. This takes us back to Professor Osberg's statement, cited at the beginning of this chapter, equating social cohesion and economic equality. Bénabou puts together many of the pieces of theory and evidence reviewed in this chapter and suggests a theory that includes public support for redistributive public finance as one of its variables.

Bénabou's "Unequal-Societies" model is based on the following elements. First, redistributive policies such as social assistance (e.g, the Child Tax Benefit), social insurance (e.g., Canada Pension Plan/Québec Pension Plan), and publicly-provided schooling, have a positive effect on well-being and growth. This is because of the presence of imperfect asset markets, as explained above. Second, the degree of political support for such policies declines as income becomes more unequally distributed. Thus, contrary to the redistributive-pressure hypothesis, over some range of inequality, increases in inequality *reduce* the political support for efficient redistribution. Bénabou explicitly builds into the model the lower level of influence of poorer and less educated voters. Putting these two elements together yields multiple equilibria of the model, a phenomenon described in Chapter 3. In one equilibrium, society tends toward high inequality and low redistribution (the US/UK pattern in recent decades); in another, society tends toward low inequality and high redistribution (the European pattern). The possibility of multiple equilibria means that two societies with fundamentally similar democratic politics and technological development might nonetheless diverge in terms of public education, health insurance, and levels of marginal tax rates.

Political support for redistribution is an indicator of national-level social cohesion; Bénabou demonstrates that this support is critically determined by economic inequality. Other measures of social cohesion are clearly affected by inequality. Knack and Keefer's statistical study of the social-cohesion payoff (see Chapter 2) sought to uncover the determinants of trust in the 29 countries in their data set. Inequality had a negative and significant effect on levels of expressed trust.

Our review of the link between inequality and growth, and of the overturning of the conventional wisdom regarding the nature of that link, provides us with at least three conclusions. First, there is ample reason to distinguish between equality and social cohesion. Second, both can have, under a variety of conditions, positive effects on investment and growth, but the effects work through different channels.

Further, a third conclusion emerges from a consideration of the evidence in this chapter. Social cohesion can, according to the definition and model presented in Chapter 3, be a feature of any group: a neighbourhood or village, a workplace, an extended family, the employees of a multinational corporation, an ethnic group, residents of a state or province, the citizens of a country, the people of the world. This generality notwithstanding, there is something special about the degree of social cohesion within a particular political jurisdiction, and especially within a nation. To the extent that social cohesion has beneficial consequences for economic success, consequences that could potentially be harnessed by policy-makers, then what matters is the level of cohesion within the jurisdiction of those policy-makers. To the extent that the level of social cohesion *responds* to policy-making, then once again, the political jurisdiction is the appropriate unit of analysis. Bénabou's "Unequal-Societies" model, in particular, proposes that political support for the policies of the welfare state has a prominent impact on national economic performance. What happens when we "scale up" from the local to the national level? We take up this question in the following chapter.

Bibliographic Notes

Lars Osberg's and John Myles's comments to the Standing Senate Committee on Social Affairs, Science and Technology are partly incorporated in that Committee's Final Report on Social Cohesion (SSCSAST, 1999), whence the comment above is drawn. Gini coefficients (and other measures of poverty inequality) for the post-Communist countries are given in Milanovic (1998). Current Gini coefficients for other countries are taken from the World Bank (1999). The voluminous empirical research on inequality is masterfully summarized by Bénabou (1996); Aghion et al. (2000) is another, more up-to-date summary.

6

Problems of Scaling-Up

The preceding chapters of this book have illustrated the considerable enthusiasm with which researchers have greeted the concept of social cohesion, and its close intellectual cousin, social capital. If my sole aim had been to document that enthusiasm, I could have gone quite a bit further. In the domain of development economics — that portion of the discipline that looks at problems of growth and inequality in the poor countries that predominate on the planet — the adoption of social capital as an analytical concept has been virtually unanimous and breathtakingly complete (at least in comparison to the uptake of other topics in the past). Harvard's Robert Putnam, a political scientist whose Italian study was glossed in Chapter 1, has become a media celebrity (at least by the standards of university professors) in the US, recounting the precipitous decline of social capital in the US. Among the chattering classes of Canada, too, social capital and social cohesion have found some purchase. *Toronto Star* economics reporter David Crane wrote a glowing account of the "discovery" of social capital by economists in March 2000. In October of that year, University of British Columbia economist John F. Helliwell — whose research on social capital has been fundamental to our evolving understanding of the material reviewed in this book — delivered a keynote address to the conservative C.D. Howe Institute in Toronto on the topic of globalization. In that lecture, he pointed to social capital as a critical variable for understanding the differences in success across economies.

But the reception accorded to social cohesion has not been universally warm. *National Post* columnist Peter Foster called Helliwell's appeal to social cohesion "woolly thinking." And in the halls of academe, some critics have likewise repudiated this new concept. Some observers find social capital to be used in nonsensical ways. Princeton University sociologists Alejandro Portes and Patricia Landolt have argued that analysts have tended to employ the term tautologically: "In the celebratory view of social capital, if an agricultural

cooperative advances economically or a city effectively carries out
a reform program, it is because they had high levels of social capital
to begin with; if they fail, they did not. This circularity of reasoning
is facilitated by the identification of the same traits as determinants
and consequences." Thus, for example, some writers consider "civic
engagement" both an independent variable that determines a
group's "success" (however measured) as well as a measure of that
success itself.

This critique is well taken, but not particularly relevant to the
economic research regarding social cohesion reviewed in Chapters 2
and 3. Take Knack and Keefer's macroeconomic statistical analysis
of the effect of trust on economic growth. There, the concept of social
cohesion — the "rate of trust" in a country — is clearly distinguished
from the measure of success — the average rate of economic growth.
Their argument is not tautological. One can quibble over whether the
rate of trust *caused* the economic growth, or whether instead some
third variable caused both the trust and the growth. But the inclusion
of other variables in a multivariate regression framework dramatically limits the likelihood of such errors of interpretation. At a more
profound level, one can argue with the assumption that "trust," as
measured in the World Values Survey, accurately measures "social
cohesion," or even more profoundly, whether economic growth is
good in the first place. But such criticisms do not impugn the methodological rigour of the study or the robustness of its results.

In addition to criticizing conceptual and methodological problems
that might afflict some of the research on social cohesion, some have
drawn attention to practical problems of the idea's application. The
political implications of an insistence on social cohesion, some have
pointed out, are ambiguous. This in itself is not a shortcoming of the
research program — the policy recommendations of many social
science research programs are ambiguous. But many of the enthusiasts of social cohesion research might be taken aback to learn some
of the lessons that policy-makers take from their results. In somewhat
stark terms, many writers on social cohesion have championed the
ability of communities to allocate resources and resolve conflicts as
an alternative to markets and commerce. Thus, people in rural communities might provide material assistance to neighbours hit by some
unforeseen hardship. This is a substitute for the market solution of
just buying an insurance policy that pays off should a hardship occur.
At the same time, however, others have seen communities as an
alternative to the state. In this case, rural dwellers' helping each other

out could be a substitute for government's social-assistance pro-grams. The two viewpoints are not mutually exclusive. When politi-cal progressives laud the legitimacy of communities, they could be reinforcing the politically conservative agenda of downsizing the state. Thus, Laurentian University economist Brian MacLean argues: "It seems that, whether consciously or not, the policy elites of the world — at the OECD and the World Bank and elsewhere — are concocting some new, centre-right encompassing, supply-side eco-nomics and adding a dash of social cohesion rhetoric to make it more palatable to the general public." Social cohesion is a long way from establishing solid left-wing or right-wing credentials, as conserva-tives like Francis Fukuyama and progressives like John Helliwell employ the term with equal vigour. This is understandably disquiet-ing for political wags on both sides of the divide.

The Downside of Social Cohesion

A second practical concern with the application of social cohesion is what has come to be termed its "downside." Shared values among the members of a group may indeed foster co-operative behaviour, but this could be a bad thing for society as a whole. Tight-knit groups could promote, successfully, anti-social behaviour like lynching. Or lots of different tight-knit groups, not necessarily anti-social per se, might nevertheless pursue internecine inter-group conflict, as with Protestants and Catholics in Ulster, or Serbs and just about everyone else in the former Yugoslavia. As Steven Durlauf, an economist from the University of Wisconsin, Madison, writes, "social mechanisms which enforce certain types of community behavior logically lead to correlated behaviors, but do not necessarily lead to socially desirable behaviors." This is not a terribly surprising discovery; indeed, it is more surprising that so few of the pioneers of social-cohesion re-search recognized this possibility. Durlauf points out that this blind spot toward abusive social cohesion stems precisely from the tauto-logical way that some researchers use the term: "By defining the presence of social capital in terms of the presence of desirable out-comes, it is of course impossible not to treat social capital as an unalloyed virtue."

The tendency to see the action of social norms in this rosy light is prevalent, for example, in the research on community management of the commons, and locally-controlled natural resource systems like fisheries or irrigation systems. Social scientists have been especially quick to point to the success of social capital in husbanding these resources. Researchers typically describe such communities quite affectionately, but this is not the only way to view them. Yale Law School professor Carol Rose, a specialist in environmental law, describes the "attractive, picturesque, and much-cited" research on the lobster gangs of Maine:

> The islanders effectively manage the lobster stock..., controlling depredation of nearby lobstering grounds by following customary norms; they allocate fishing rights among themselves and use informal punishment to defend the "perimeter" of their fishing grounds from outsiders ... In a somewhat flintier light, however, these same lobster fishermen appear to be much less attractive: they look xenophobic, hierarchical, thuggish, and thoroughly misogynist.

Portes and Landolt, the Princeton sociologists, have perhaps done the most to argue the downside of social cohesion. The pursuit of the public bad, rather than the public good, by groups is not only a bad thing in itself, but can be expected to have negative repercussions, including economic ones. They identify at least three variants of this negative effect. First, some groups organize precisely to predate upon the larger society, or at the very least to seek gains that come at the expense of some other group or groups. They point out that some ethnic groups essentially control access to the construction trades and to fire and police unions in New York City, for example, excluding others. There are certainly other, similar, examples in many North American cities. Second, groups restrict individual freedom among their ranks. The adherence to a "social standard of behaviour," discussed in Chapter 3, almost by definition constrains individual agency. As Portes and Landolt put it: "In small towns, all your neighbors may know you, and you can get supplies on credit at the corner store. The claustrophobia, however, may be asphyxiating to the individual spirit, which is why the independent-minded have always sought to escape from these conditions and so much modern thought has celebrated the freedom of urban life." During my upbringing, there seemed to be a surfeit of movies, many of them made for TV, recounting the struggle of a misunderstood and ostracized adolescent in a narrow-minded small town; misunderstood, because he or she was secretly gay, a world-class athlete, a painter, or a firebrand unwelcome in the closely circumscribed ambit of the community. (Or maybe there weren't so many of those movies, and I was just overly responsive to the theme!) A third negative mechanism is that rigid norms might enforce "downward levelling pressures": inner-city youth dissuaded from excelling academically in favour of "keeping it real."

One of the most damning examples of correlated but socially injurious social standards of behaviour is racism in the US South. Mississippi novelist William Faulkner, among the most sensitive, if somewhat eccentric, observers of the phenomenon, often turns to the theme of racism as it is lived every day, almost exclusively among whites. This lengthy soliloquy by Lawyer Stevens, from the novel *Intruder in the Dust*, comments on one Mr. Lilley's response to the alleged murder of a white man by Lucas, a black man.

> He [Mr. Lilley] has nothing against what he calls niggers. If you ask him, he will probably tell you he likes them even better than some white folks he knows and he will believe it. They are probably constantly beating him out of a few cents here and there in his store and probably even picking up things — packages of chewing gum or bluing or a banana or a can of sardines or a pair of shoelaces or a bottle of hair-straightener — under their coats and aprons and he knows it; he probably even gives them things free of charge — the bones and spoiled meat out of his butcher's icebox and spoiled candy and lard. All he requires is that they act like niggers. Which is exactly what Lucas is doing: blew his top and murdered a white man — which Mr. Lilley is probably convinced all Negroes want to do — and now the white people will take him out and burn him, all regular and in order and themselves acting exactly as he is convinced Lucas would wish them to act: like white folks; both of them observing implicitly the rules: the nigger acting like a nigger and the white folks acting like white folks and no real hard feelings on either side ... once the fury is over; in fact Mr. Lilley would probably be one of the first to contribute cash money toward Lucas' funeral and the support of his widow and children if he had them. Which proves again how no man can cause more grief than that one clinging blindly to the vices of his ancestors.

Decades later, another great Mississippi novelist would (almost explicitly) make the link between a racist standard of behaviour and dramatically unsatisfactory economic performance. Alice Walker:

Living as I was in Mississippi it was easy to see how racist violence sapped the strength and creativity of the entire population. Mississippi was the poorest state in the nation not because of the federal government's meddling in its affairs, beginning with the Civil War, as white apologists for the state's poverty at the drop of a hat exclaimed, but because every tiny surplus of energy not used in immediate living day-to-day was put into maintaining a hypocritical, artificial and basically untenable separation of the races, with domination of black people attained through violence.

Successful collective action can be ruinous; shared standards of behaviour can be deadly. This is not a theoretical curiosity, but a real consequence of group behaviour. Xenophobic, hierarchical, thuggish, and thoroughly misogynist, indeed. From this, many conclude that social cohesion is decidedly not a good thing; others, that it is of ambiguous moral value.

Much of the confusion regarding whether social cohesion is a good or bad thing, or whether it is productive, unproductive, or counterproductive, stems, I think, from confusion regarding the unit of analysis. Does social cohesion deliver for the groups that have it? Most commentators would say yes. (But I will say no, sometimes, below.) Social psychologists argue that urban gangs offer otherwise disaffected youths opportunities for belonging, fellow feeling, dignity, and self-determination. Less socially-excluded people can derive these benefits from their inclusion in the liberal nation-state. For the disadvantaged young person in a dangerous urban neighbourhood, perhaps, belonging to a gang confers certain human benefits, more so than any other of the bleak options on offer. Is the kid better off this way? Possibly so. Is this good for the neighbourhood, for kids in other gangs, for the city as a whole? No, but we were talking about the gang and its members, not outsiders.

The theory of social cohesion outlined in this book suggests that groups whose members invest in social capital are better poised to co-operate to pursue collective aims. Co-operation within the group is a sort of victory that many groups or potential groups fail to achieve. Nothing about this requires that the group's objective is a socially benign one. So it is with street gangs, whose objectives are almost precisely defined in terms of defeating the objectives of other street gangs. In fact, this propensity of tight-knit groups to predate upon the larger society or upon groups within it has a long, if irregular, history in economic theory. The late Mancur Olson, in his classic exposition on collective action, hypothesized that successful groups were most likely to be those with a narrow interest not shared by society at large. Going back quite a bit further, Adam Smith famously remarked that, "People of the same trade seldom meet together, even for merriment and diversion, but the conversation ends in a conspiracy against the public, or in some contrivance to raise prices."

There is nothing newsworthy, then, or remarkable, about these points. But there is a logical non sequitur in many criticisms of social cohesion. Proponents of the usefulness of social cohesion will say: "Social cohesion brings benefits to the group that possesses it." Detractors say, "Some groups harm others." There is no inconsistency between these statements, and the latter statement does nothing to disprove the former.

But there is a further undesirable aspect to some cohesive groups. Whether or not they harm outsiders, Portes and Landolt's asphyxiating small towns do harm to *insiders*. That is, some or all members of some groups might be better off in the absence of the group's social cohesion. This is the startling part of Walker's description of Mississippi: in a very real sense, racist whites themselves would be better off with a rearrangement of social reality. Even if they remained racist, their incomes might be sufficiently higher to compensate them! How could the members of a group adhere to a social standard of behaviour (as the concept was defined in Chapter 3) that harmed them individually?

Here it is useful to underscore the difference between collective and individual rationality. Adherence to a positively injurious social standard of behaviour might be the individually rational thing to do, given that everyone else is doing it too. This does not preclude the possibility that the standard of behaviour in question is not collectively rational: it is possible that many or all members of the group would be better off with some different standard of behaviour. But no one faces an incentive, *individually*, to deviate. History is fraught with examples of collectively irrational behaviour by individually rational people. Newfoundland cod fishermen would have all been better off, in the long run, with lower fishing yields; given what every other fisherman was doing, however, no one fisherman would have gained from unilaterally cutting back. In the collective adherence to social standards of behaviour, the critical point is that successful standards are self-enforcing in this way.

To push this point even further, it is possible that there is another *equilibrium* where everyone, or at least many members of society, would be happier. This is a consequence of the multiple equilibria of the social cohesion model in Chapter 3. But there might be no obvious way to get from the bad equilibrium to the good one. At times, in contrast to the words of Faulkner's Lawyer Stevens, people cling not blindly, but coolly and rationally, to the vices of their ancestors.

The Scaling-Up Problem

For many, debate surrounding the "downside" of social cohesion, especially among academics, ends there. Many define social cohesion as a good thing. Period. Others identify these socially pathological behaviours and declare the enthusiasm for social cohesion to be misguided. Period. But for many others, there is something analytically useful, and perhaps even something politically attractive, about the concept that persuades us to dig deeper.

Many of the issues related to the "downside debate" have to do with the problem of "scaling up." After all, much of the good news regarding social cohesion has to do with comparing the effects of different levels of trust in, say, France to trust in Germany. (Refer to Table 1.1 to refresh your memory on the levels of trust in these and other countries.) In contrast, in this book we have tended to view social cohesion as arising from the interactions of many people all over the world — whether random, impersonal interactions, or close-knit, multidimensional relationships. Pockets of social cohesion can emerge in some settings, and will fail to do so elsewhere. But when we start to talk about abstractions like "the level of social cohesion in Canada," this highly decentralized, bottom-up, view of social cohesion does not quite fit. It might make sense to talk about "the level of social cohesion" in Advocate Harbour, Nova Scotia, or in The Annex in Toronto, but how do we scale up to Canada as a whole?

In fact, many of the national-level counter-examples of social cohesion gone awry (Ulster, Yugoslavia) are really examples of failures of local-level cohesion to scale up. Of course, another logical possibility is that close-knit local centres of cohesion will simply not interact at all. The issue was considered by Lord Durham in his report on Upper Canada in the wake of the Mackenzie rebellion of 1838:

The Province has no great centre with which all the separate parts are connected, and which they are accustomed to follow in sentiment and action: nor is there that habitual intercourse between the inhabitants of different parts of the country, which ... makes a people one and united ... Instead of this, there are many petty local centres, the sentiments and the interests ... of which, are distinct and perhaps opposed.

A province might contain vibrant communities, all of which achieve good equilibria, and yet remain completely separate if there is no mechanism to aggregate local-level cohesion, no "habitual intercourse" to unify "sentiments and interests." Indeed, returning to the international differences in expressed levels of trust in others displayed in Table 1.1, one might be struck by the low ranking of Brazil, Turkey, and Mexico. These countries are full of rural communities with dense social networks that can facilitate co-operation for better economic outcomes; these are precisely the kind of societies most development economists have in mind when they think of social cohesion. One explanation for their low ranking, of course, in the results of the World Values Survey is that these countries comprise little poles of social cohesion whose radii are very restricted. (There are certainly other factors as well. All three countries may contain cohesive — if hierarchical and misogynist — village societies, but they also contain many impersonal large cities, and it was city dwellers who were disproportionately represented in the World Values Survey. And in light of the link between social cohesion and income inequality discussed in Chapter 5, it is worthwhile to point out that Mexico and Brazil are among the most unequal economies in the world today.) Moreover, in the presence of multiple equilibria, there is no guarantee that local cohesion will scale up. That is, some communities might sustain co-operative behaviour, while others are marked by universally unco-operative behaviour.

But countries might nevertheless have mechanisms of "habitual intercourse" that facilitate scaling up. Groups share geographic and political space. In terms of the social cohesion model of Chapter 3, suppose that the level of social cohesion — the payoff to mutual co-operation — is determined by social-capital investments throughout society. But suppose that people only interact within restricted groups; they are only matched with like people. Then, a group with an initially low level of social cohesion could generate co-operative behaviour, provided the initial level of social cohesion in the other group is sufficiently high. By the same token, a group that initially exhibits co-operative behaviour might cease to do so if the other group does not.

Suppose for example that two irrigating villages are adjacent to each other (or that a single village comprises members of two caste groups). Social-capital investments in each village take the form of resources sacrificed to organization and co-ordination of common tasks like canal cleaning; co-operation takes the form of the canal-cleaning work itself. The level of social cohesion in each village is the depreciated stock of all social-capital investments made in that village: the number of hours, suitably depreciated, spent planning and co-ordinating over the years. But the rate of return to mutual co-operation among each neighbouring pair of farmers depends on the level of social cohesion in *both* villages. If both villages draw water from the same reservoir, this spillover is easy to understand: one village's co-operative success affects the level of water available, which in turn affects the incentives toward co-operation in the other village. Alternatively, both villages might draw water from the same government-administered main canal (as is commonly the case in India) and cleaning of canals by one village will increase the flow of water to the other. In any case, the two segments of society are linked through the physical interrelatedness of the irrigation-canal network.

Or it could be that two workplaces that service aircraft generate social cohesion as discussed earlier: attending training sessions and similar activities is a social-capital investment that signals to your co-workers that you plan to work hard in the future. The rate of return to mutual co-operation following social-capital investment, however, depends on the level of cohesion at *both* work sites. These could be two aircraft servicing facilities at two different airports. Given that they work on the same airplanes, the return to high effort at one airport rises when the level of effort expended by workers at the other airport rises as well.

In both cases, high levels of co-operation in one subgroup "infect" the other subgroup. Alternatively, it could be that both subgroups have sufficiently high initial levels of social cohesion, but one sub-group's unco-operative behaviour undermines co-operation in the other. But what if there are no automatic linkages like a shared canal or a common aircraft? People in a nation, even if they hardly share geographic or cultural space, share fiscal space: they are all, in theory at least, subject to a single regime of taxation and other government policies. The following chapter will explore ways in which this common experience of policy can foster social cohesion.

Moreover, national borders can co-ordinate people's behaviour just because everyone can see them. If it is widely believed that there is more trust in Canada than in the US, then a person crossing the border northward might be willing to engage in certain co-operative behaviours from which she is dissuaded in the US, even though there is no change in her psychology. Her strategies are simply conditioned by her environment. In much the same vein, a rational Canadian, having rented a car at Heathrow airport, will drive into London on the left side of the road, even though she would never do so at home.

National Cohesion

The real issue is not whether social cohesion can sometimes be a bad thing, but rather the conditions under which what's good for groups turns out to be good for the common weal as well. A key distinction is between intragroup dynamics for any group (which might be a street gang) and intragroup dynamics where the group in question is a viable polity, like a city, province or nation-state. Street gangs might exhibit high degrees of internal cohesion and provide a psychological sense of belonging and connectedness to their members, and they might successfully mobilize to achieve shared goals, but frequently at the expense of other street gangs and the society at large. Policy-makers, however, in the first instance must be concerned with instilling or facilitating social cohesion at the level of the nation-state. There is good reason to focus not on the street-gang variant of social cohesion, and instead look at the question of successful scaling up to the nation-state.

Why the nation-state? This might seem a somewhat arbitrary distinction, and in some ways it is. If we care about economic systems, we must acknowledge that economic trading networks are not wholly bounded within national borders. But even there, the nation-state continues to be massively relevant. As John McCallum and, more recently, John Helliwell have shown, interprovincial trade flows in Canada are still much larger than province-to-US trade. Helliwell gives the example of trade flows between Ontario and British Columbia and California. One might expect Ontario's trade with California to be roughly ten times as large as its trade with British Columbia, since California has about ten times the population of British Columbia (and hence roughly ten times the buying power), while California and British Columbia are equally distant from Ontario. But in fact Ontario's trade with British Columbia is not one tenth of its California trade: Ontario trades more with British Columbia.

In fact, the key question is, what is the largest unit at which, in practice, social cohesion is exhibited? If it scales up to the nation, that is not just a nice coincidence. In that case, social cohesion coincides with the dimensions of a polity that has a lot of levers available to it — public policy — not necessarily available to other scales of society (communities, neighbourhoods, municipalities, the world). Accordingly, the following chapter will consider how a consciousness of social cohesion changes our views about policy-making.

Bibliographic Notes

Brian MacLean is cited from his always-informative Web site covering "Canada's Economy in the Newspapers" (MacLean, 2000). Durlauf's (1999) critique of social capital appeared in the newsletter of the University of Wisconsin's Institute for Research on Poverty, where it was accompanied by a "pro" social capital piece, also well worth reading, by economist Samuel Bowles. Université de Montréal sociologist Paul Bernard (1999) raises the concern that local level social cohesion — in a workplace, for example — can lead to undesirable intergroup competition. Portes and Landolt's 1996 piece in *The American Prospect*, cited here, can be supplemented by more academic versions of their argument, in Portes (1998) and Portes and Landolt (2000). The Faulkner passage is from *Intruder in the Dust*, pp. 48-49. The citation from Alice Walker is taken from a special 1988 Afterword to her 1970 novel *The Third Life of Grange Copeland*, p. 344. Both the novel and the later Afterword are worth a read. The essay is a commentary on the genesis of the novel, her first, but speaks more generally to some of the dominant themes in Walker's oeuvre, notably the niceties of battling sexism and racism at the same time. Adam Smith is again cited from the Canaan edition of *The Wealth of Nations*, p. 148 (Bk. I, Ch. X, Pt. I). The Durham report is cited in Wynn (1987, pp. 265–266). The microeconomic logic of the scaling-up problem is considered in greater detail in Dayton-Johnson (forthcoming). Evidence on Canadian-US trade flows is analyzed in McCallum (1995), and Helliwell (1998). Helliwell considers the Ontario-BC-California example in his 2000 C.D. Howe Institute Benefactors Lecture.

7

Policies for Cohesion

Let's take stock. Social cohesion is the result of social-capital investments by individuals, and is reflected best perhaps by a society's
associational life and the degree of trust among its members. Societies where people are members of many overlapping groups, where
civil society thickens, where trust among family members general-
izes to trust of strangers, enjoy better economic performance. There
is ample room still for debate about whether social networks or the
level of trust is truly "capital," about the relative contribution to
economic performance of social capital compared to physical capital
or human capital, about the "downside" of social cohesion. But it is
fair to say that consensus is forming around the idea that "social
cohesion matters" for economic performance in the modern capitalist
economy.

Practically-minded readers will push this conclusion a bit. Does
this recognition that social cohesion is a critical part of economic
success merely provide a more nuanced view of how economies
function? Is this only a philosophical discussion of the frontier between market and non-market kinds of social interactions? Or, more
concretely, does it change the way we think about policy-making?
Does a consciousness of and sensitivity toward social cohesion
change the kinds of policies we would recommend for economic
prosperity?

For a lot of writers, no policy message emerges from a reasoned
consideration of social cohesion. Thus, Francis Fukuyama, the conservative political scientist, writes that while a vibrant civil society
is necessary for economic success, it is largely beyond the reach of
policy-making: civil society "depends on people's habits, customs,
and ethics — attributes that can be shaped only indirectly through
conscious political action and must otherwise be nourished through
an increased awareness and respect for culture" (1995, p. 5). Political
scientist Robert Putnam argues that the decline in American social
capital over the last quarter century is sufficiently critical that poli-

ticians should start thinking seriously about it. Nevertheless, his account of local democracy in Italy leaves the sympathetic policy-maker empty-handed if she is seeking policy lessons. A vertically-oriented Catholic social hierarchy stifled rich associational life in the South, while an enterprising mercantile society encouraged horizontal links in the North. A fascinating history, but one that appears remarkably distant from the levers of public policy. How could tax policy or monetary policy, say, have any kind of impact over a short-term political horizon, in the face of thousands of years of history?

This policy pessimism, one could argue, stems from a more general antipathy toward looking to the government to redress social ills. Those hostile to government intervention in the economy will not be sanguine regarding government intervention to build social cohesion. I do not share that antipathy, but a cursory look at the theory of social cohesion outlined in this book, particularly in Chapter 3, provides a sizeable boost to the pessimist's view. Some societies have a large initial endowment of social cohesion, which favours co-operative behaviour, and this tendency is self-reinforcing: co-operation begets further co-operation. Because of the possibility of multiple equilibria, some societies might early on deplete stocks of social capital and this tendency, too, is self-reinforcing: unco-operative behaviour begets unco-operative behaviour. Certain social standards of behaviour — a feature of "community," in the parlance of Chapter 3 — are self-enforcing promoters of the co-operative behaviour that is necessary for economic success. How can an appropriate standard of behaviour be instilled where one is absent? It is ludicrous to suppose that government can simply tell people to behave and be done with it.

Having said all this, there are good reasons to suspect that policy-making can affect social cohesion. First of all, many would acknowledge that certain types of policies can weaken or destroy social cohesion. Divisive politics, government in the name of a particular group, using the machinery of government to systematically disfavour other groups; such phenomena are not unknown and by just about any definition of social cohesion must unravel knitted warmth. More subtle, perhaps, are critiques that claim that unbridled liberalization, particularly the "Washington Consensus" brand preached by the World Bank and IMF in the poor countries of the world, can weaken social cohesion. By increasing economic insecurity, by encouraging the fleet-footed movement of capital and labour, such "market-friendly" policies weaken habitual modes of interaction and loosen the bonds that undergird social standards of behaviour. The frustrating conclusion of this school of thought, however, is that, as policy recommendation, it is merely proscriptive. "Do not govern divisively." "Do not liberalize in an unbridled fashion." These are not helpful tips.

That there may be a positive policy lesson — "do this," not only "do NOT do that" — from the study of social cohesion seems a lot more likely if one considers the phenomenon of *corporate culture.* Firms, and not only large firms, devote considerable energy and resources to the cultivation and maintenance of a corporate culture. This is quite solidly akin to the airplane hangar, our running work- place example of social cohesion. What is corporate culture? Busi- ness schools instruct prospective managers in the skills of fostering a group identity and creating reasonable expectations of co-opera- tion. Workplaces have softball teams, retreats, seminars, casual days, birthday parties. What purpose could such activities possibly serve in the pursuit of delivering value to shareholders? Perhaps managers were early recruits to the view that (probably a slightly cynical brand of) social cohesion can promote economic success. If employers believe they can tinker with the social environment of the workplace to build what are essentially social standards of behaviour (in the sense of Chapter 3) for the society of the workplace, could not government promote trust in the society of the whole? The analogy suggests a broad scope for policy-making to contribute to social cohesion, which will in turn favour investment and growth in the economy.

There are important differences between polities and firms, of course. Some of these differences underscore the practical signifi- cance of differentiating between social cohesion on the job (or among the members of an ethnic group, say) and social cohesion at the level of the political jurisdiction. In the first place, decision-making in the modern liberal democracy is a lot more, well, democratic, than in just about any private firm. Imposing values and views on the work- place may be legal and even morally acceptable in a wide variety of situations (even while, in cases like systematic sexual harassment, it is neither) even if many employees do not enthusiastically share those views and values. However, attempts by well-meaning govern- ments to inculcate values not generally shared by the populace will be problematic at best. Second, no one is excluded from the liberal democracy. Or, more accurately, the liberal democracy can legiti- mately be brought to task, under its own rules of conduct, if it systematically trammels the interests of a particular class or group. Not so workplaces. Firms are legally prevented from practising many types of discrimination, but not from dismissing an employee who is not a "team player," who refuses to adopt, at least while she is at work, the corporate culture. In the public sphere, if schools expel "troubled" children or hospitals turn away patients, there is an understandable hue and cry to the effect that the state does not have the option of selectively excluding certain classes of citizens. The third point is the converse of the previous one. Just as the polity cannot, ideally, "fire" eccentrics and dissidents, neither can people "quit." Of course, people move across international borders every day in the thousands, as legal and illegal immigrants, as political and economic refugees. Some of those cases are like "quitting" the country analogously to quitting a firm: they are driven by differences of opinion regarding the project of society. Others are a different kind of flight, generally guided by economic need. For many, probably most, Canadians, "exit" is a drastic and last-resort kind of political statement. Moving to another country is a more costly and difficult transition, by several orders of magnitude, than switching jobs. The virtual impossibility of a democratic state firing one of its citizens, and the practical difficulty of a citizen of such a state quitting her country means in practice that democracies will be populated by a much wider variety of people than a firm. A wider array of values and views must be accommodated and respected in the polity. The workplace, meanwhile, will tend to evolve toward a much greater uniformity of vision. All of these differences mean that a straightforward application of the "corporate culture" model to inculcating social cohesion in Canada today is bound to founder on several fronts.

The remainder of this chapter surveys a series of "snapshots" of policy arenas where a consciousness of social cohesion changes the way we think about policy-making. These brief vignettes are not meant to be definitive policy statements. The emphasis is Canadian, although the more general lessons are applicable to a wide variety of advanced industrial economies. This kind of inquiry would be quite different, and quite fascinating, for economies that differ substantially from Canada's — Mexico, Vietnam, Ukraine, Sierra Leone. I will only say about poorer countries (and lower income than Canada is about the *only* thing the four countries listed above have in common) that social cohesion is equally critical to their economic development. It is not an extravagance that only rich countries can afford. Moreover, as such countries weather far more rapid and far-reaching structural changes than today's wealthy countries ever did, they must tend with special care their precarious stocks of knitted warmth.

Regional Mobility and Children

Something missing from my simple model of social cohesion is *learning*. People in a cohesive society learn to interact differently. They learn to trust each other, and that trust could be habit forming. Nowhere in society is the process of learning to be co-operative and connected more salient than among children. Adults may or may not learn to be more co-operative as societies evolve; children, as a matter of course, develop new behaviour and tendencies with an alacrity and élan that is the source of both wonderment and consternation for their parents. Thus the evolution of a society in a direction of greater co-operative behaviour, in addition to having effects on economic performance, has dynamic effects through society's influence on its children. And in general, social scientists and policy-makers have long agreed that providing a rich and secure environment for parents to raise children has tremendous benefits, economic and otherwise, for society when those children reach adulthood. Conversely, trauma, want, and misery during childhood create deficits that those children, once grown, may never overcome. Economist Shelley Phipps of Dalhousie University argues that this conventional view of "investing" in children, while plausible as far as it goes, should be superseded by a "child-centred" view of children's welfare. What matters for society is not only how well the children will get on when they grow up, but how well off they are today. Children account for a quarter of Canadian society; any reasonable estimate of the level of Canadian well-being must pay special attention to the factors that make children happy and healthy right now.

Much recent research demonstrates the quite dramatic effects on psycho-social outcomes for children, as children, of disturbances in their family life. Beyond the well-known detrimental effects of household violence or divorce, a household's economic behaviour and circumstances have important, and often harmful, effects on children. Professor Phipps has shown, using Canadian data, that the effect on children's anxiety of moving the household is similar in magnitude to the effect of having an unemployed parent, or being exposed to a spell of poverty. There are many reasons why this might be so; the trauma of radically changing one's life circumstances, one's house, one's neighbourhood, one's school, and most important, one's incipient network of friends and teachers and others, is terribly upsetting to a child.

This is tremendously important in Canada, where mobility of people among regions is higher than in any other developed country. Canadians are footloose to a degree that surpasses even that of Americans. In many ways, this is a good thing: it demonstrates that Canadians are quick to respond to changing economic circumstances, to go where the jobs are, where opportunities present themselves. A less mobile country would have a less productive economy. But Phipps's research shows that this can have harmful effects on childhood development that have, in turn, counterproductive economic consequences. Children grow up more anxious, with greater probability of various illnesses such as asthma. This is harmful to their productivity and well-being. More generally, these children grow up less attached to a larger community, and less likely to feel a part of a larger connected whole. They are less likely to have internalized the norms and codes of conduct that underly the cohesive economy. Now as a society, Canadians may decide that the negative impact of high regional mobility on children is far outweighed by other economic benefits of that mobility. There are always trade-offs in economic affairs. But nevertheless, without a consciousness of social cohesion, and its importance to childhood development, we will make decisions regarding regional mobility without full information about its consequences.

The Governor General's Throne Speech in October 1999 bespoke a renewed commitment on the part of the Chrétien government to the well-being of children. In light of the importance of social cohesion to children's well-being and development, one could call on the Canadian government to seriously address the impacts of regional mobility. How can this be accomplished? The most efficacious mechanism is to temper the economic imperative to move for those lower-income families most pushed by economic factors. (Lower-income families, moreover, already have several social counts against them in the effort to provide a secure home for their children, as they seek to stretch scarce resources.) The economic push can be mitigated by more generous Employment Insurance benefits. The trend of the last twenty years has been to restrict eligibility for EI, to the point where currently only 30 percent of the unemployed receive benefits at all. When parents lose their jobs, more generous EI might temper their decision to move thousands of kilometres. More generally, a renewed commitment to interprovincial equalization transfers

— federally directed transfers of general tax revenue from more to less prosperous provinces in Canada — will ensure that the imperative to leave is not so great for families that would like to stay.

Community Economic Development

To this must be added investment incentive to foster community economic development in traditionally depressed regions that tend to witness outflows of families. This is particularly the case in areas where seasonal economic activities like fishing have created great economic strains and where eligibility for social assistance has been most drastically curtailed.

While community-economic-development projects could be justified in order to reduce the pressure on families, there are additional grounds to reconsider this economic strategy. What, indeed, is the rationale behind community economic development? In addition to acute need in depressed regions, there is some notion that communities have some resources upon which to draw, resources that might not be available to all local economies. That stock of resources can plausibly be called social cohesion. The co-operative backdrop for economic success might be sturdier in small towns and rural regions: smaller populations and therefore more multidimensional relationships, longer historical memory, shared vulnerability to resource-based economies (farming, forestry, fishing, mining, etc.) are all factors that might create communities of shared values and interpretation.

Indeed, survey evidence demonstrates that rural Canadians generally evince higher levels of social capital and social cohesion than their urban counterparts. In a separate research project, I analyzed Canadian responses to the World Values Survey to assess the relative importance of various characteristics (e.g., income, education, age, province, and rural or urban residence) in determining associational activity and levels of trust. In short, does rural Canada exhibit more social cohesion than urban Canada, controlling for many other factors? The answer is yes, usually.

Table 7.1 summarizes some information regarding rural/urban differences in associational life in Canada. The average number of groups to which a person belongs, or for which a person performs unpaid work, is higher among rural Canadians than urban Canadians. The lower half of the table gives some regression coefficients from a pair of multivariate statistical models. For example, in the first column, the model estimates the determinants of the number of groups to which every survey respondent belongs; the results give us the relative contribution of a large number of factors, including age, income, educational attainment, and province of residence. Reproduced in Table 7.1 is the relative contribution of a household's rural status. This means that, controlling for a large number of other variables, a rural Canadian is, on average, a member of 0.56 more groups than her urban Canadian counterpart. Given that the average number of group memberships nationwide is about 1.7, the "rural effect" on group membership is quite sizeable. Similarly, controlling for other characteristics, a rural Canadian volunteers for 0.66 more groups than a urban counterpart. (Table 7.1 also reports two regional indicators from the study summarized here: the rural-Saskatchewan and the rural-Newfoundland effects. In both cases, people in rural Saskatchewan exhibit substantially less associational activity than others, again controlling for many other variables, while rural Newfoundlanders exhibit substantially more such activity. Both results are statistically significant, and similar negative "rural-SK effects" and positive "rural-NF effects" recurred in other analysis in the study.)

Table 7.1. Associational Activity, Rural and Urban Canada

	Groups to which you belong ...	Groups for which you volunteer ...
Rural Canada	1.93	1.37
Urban Canada	1.59	0.81
All	1.71	0.97
Selected Regression Coefficients		
Rural	0.560	0.655
Rural SK	-1.17	-1.36
Rural NF	1.79	2.68

The top half of the table shows average numbers of groups for each category; the bottom half gives selected regression coefficients. Source: Dayton-Johnson (2000a).

Rural Canadians are significantly more likely to trust others generally, although they are no more likely than urban Canadians to trust other Canadians or their own family members. Rural respondents express lower levels of trust in speakers of the other official language and in recent immigrants to Canada; these results are marginally significant, but below the usual 90 percent cutoff. These results are nevertheless important, given that they suggest that while rural Canada might exhibit higher levels of social cohesion, the radius of trust is more circumscribed there. The quick summary of this research is that there is more social capital in rural Canada than elsewhere, as measured by group membership and voluntary activity. Moreover, rural Canadians are significantly more likely to agree that "most people can be trusted."

If one accepts that, all else being equal, more social capital will tend to favour economic activity, then there is solid evidence that $1 of public investment in rural Canada might yield a higher return than $1 invested in urban Canada. Of course, all else does not remain equal. Despite its social-capital advantage, rural Canada might not measure up to many urban areas in terms of physical and human capital, which are similarly indispensable for creating returns on investment. Moreover, this book's explicit recognition of multiple equilibria is a cautionary tale. Not all rural regions will necessarily be rich stores of social capital.

Groupes Communautaires and Voluntarism

If we believe that it is really people's membership in voluntary organizations of all kinds that constitutes social cohesion, then policies for a cohesive economy must somehow make it easier for people to find enriching opportunities to join such groups. A direct way is for government to support community organizations with financial and in-kind resources. The Parti Québécois government, returned to power in Québec in 1994, promised to do just that. In November 1999, representatives of a wide array of *groupes communautaires* — involved in activities ranging from literacy, care for the sick in their homes, and helping people return to employment — rallied in Québec City to remind the Bouchard government of its promise.

Many commentators are enthusiastic about the potential for voluntary organizations providing basic social services usually entrusted to the welfare state — delivering meals to the elderly and the disabled, caring for children of working parents, providing services to the homeless and the poor, for example. Volunteers are frequently motivated and energetic and can respond quite flexibly to the changing needs of those they serve, perhaps in ways that government bureaucracies can do only at high cost. US President George Bush's call in his 1989 inaugural address for "a thousand points of light" looked forward to a flowering of precisely this kind of voluntary effort to care for America's less fortunate.

At the same time, others worry that Bush *père*'s initiative and others like it represent a shirking of the state's responsibility, and an attempt to transfer the formidable burden of caring for the less fortunate — the poor, the aged, the unemployed, the disabled — onto the shoulders of a dedicated but overburdened core of private citizens. And there are sound economic reasons to suspect that the private supply of social assistance will always be lower than the level that society would like. I may, as a private citizen, sincerely wish to provide for those in need, but as long as someone else is looking after it, I have very little incentive to contribute money or time. Or I may despair that my contribution is a drop in the bucket next to the magnitude of the problems to be addressed. If I contribute by means of my taxes, conversely, then I am paying my fair share, and my drop in the bucket is combined with literally thousands of other drops into a significant amount.

While economists and policy-makers debate how to harness the motivation and energy of volunteers without abandoning the state's commitment to those in need, the Péquiste government has actually offered a pragmatic and delightfully simple way out of this impasse. Why not just pay the groups that exist, freeing up volunteers' time from fundraising and assuring the groups that they will have stability over the next few years — stability that translates into security both for volunteers and for the public they serve. Some 500 *groupes communautaires* share $300-million annually, a portion of which is provided by Loto-Québec. Meanwhile, the provincial government continues to provide many complementary services on its own.

This is not to say that the Québec model is without flaws — indeed, the rallying of members of *groupes communautaires* indicates a sluggishness of the Québec government in delivering on its promises. Moreover, it is not clear that the division of responsibilities between *groupes communautaires* and government bureaucracies is necessarily the most efficient. But it is a straightforward way to facilitate the stability and success of service organizations that, in addition to providing social assistance, generate social capital among their members and social cohesion for the society as a whole. Carleton University economist Frances Woolley has studied the relative strengths of governmental versus non-governmental provision of social assistance and charity in Canada. Based on evidence from the 1997 National Survey of Giving, Volunteering and Participating (NSGVP) in Canada, Woolley finds some confirmation that volunteers in Canada evince higher levels of trust in others than those who do not volunteer. She does not, however, find strong links between volunteering and other measures of cohesion: shared values or social tolerance. Woolley further worries that enthusiasm for voluntary provision, rather than public provision, of social assistance will have disappointing consequences. For policy-makers the question should not be public versus private provision, she argues; it should be, rather, which services make sense in the public sphere and which make sense in the private sphere? She suggests that private volunteers are good at providing high-quality and personalized service in small quantities. Examples include staffing suicide-prevention hotlines or visiting senior citizens. Calling upon the volunteer sector to provide services with very different characteristics runs the risk of insufficient quantity of services, discrimination in who gets served, and rapidly depleting volunteer motivation. Such is the case of food banks and various charitably-provided services for the homeless. The Québec experience illustrates that there is at least one other option to consider: some services can be privately provided and publicly funded.

Labour Standards

Direct funding of *groupes communautaires* is not the only way to favour the voluntary association of citizens. Indeed, in a country where the population is as mobile as Canada's, the scope for promoting long-lasting local organizations might be limited; members move too frequently. (Among francophones in Québec, mobility out of province is far lower, and therefore the PQ solution detailed above might be especially fruitful in ways it wouldn't be elsewhere.) There are, however, other policies. Consider policies that govern the workplace and working conditions.

Working Canadians are concerned not only that their incomes are insufficient and precarious, but, increasingly, that their time is not their own. The new, flexible labour markets that might be associated with a relatively more productive economy take an increasing toll on workers. One way this is manifested is in day-to-day uncertainty about when shifts will be scheduled. Similar problems are faced by the growing number of workers employed as independent contractors.

Some of the more noteworthy labour struggles of the 1990s in North America reflect this issue. A review of the strike actions called by the United Auto Workers (UAW) in the US, for example, reveals that the single most important issue was probably *outsourcing*, the growing practice among automobile manufacturers of moving more and more of their production to non-union facilities. What is remarkable is that concern over outsourcing is closely followed in importance by concern over overtime, especially compulsory overtime. Eleven thousand five hundred UAW members in General Motors's Flint, Michigan facility walked out over the issue of overtime in September 1994, successfully compelling the auto producer to hire 779 new workers. Major UAW strike actions against GM in Janesville, Wisconsin in November 1996, and in Fort Wayne, Indiana in March 1997 were primarily motivated by workers fed up with compulsory overtime and insecurity about their schedules. Even though many workers are paid higher overtime rates, General Motors and other firms find it less costly to overwork existing employees than to recruit and train a larger number of workers.

Flexibility in scheduling work shifts may make firms more responsive to market conditions and hence more profitable. But it creates costs for social cohesion. Workers faced with insecure, intense, and erratic work schedules are not well poised to participate in the various organizations of civil society that strengthen social cohesion. They cannot reliably commit time and resources to voluntary associations. There has been little change in the average number of hours worked per week for every Canadian worker, but there have been, in recent years, alarming divergences among workers: many more are working fifty or more hours per week or twenty or fewer hours per week, than in decades past.

Labour standards, universally applied, that increase security and reduce intensity for workers could, accordingly, foster civic engagement and social cohesion. In the late 1990s, Ontario unions and community groups identified a "desirable dozen" new labour standards; most were intended to address this simultaneous "casualization" and "intensification" of work. Among the recommendations is the hardly controversial "8 hour day and 40 hour week": this recommendation *is* controversial nonetheless, given that General Motors sought a 56-hour work week, and the Ontario Government's "Red Tape Commission" identified 50 hours as a reasonable target. (It should be noted that Ontario does not forbid employers or employees from working more than these amounts, it merely stipulates that overtime rates must be paid above the threshold.) The niceties of these debates are crucial for social cohesion. Ontario's 2000 Employment Standards Act allows working hours to be averaged over four weeks. Now someone who works 80 hours a week, two weeks in a row, then sits at home for two weeks waiting for his next shift assignment, will earn no overtime pay. This approach is critically wrong headed from the perspective of social cohesion. These are new rallying cries for organized labour, and opportunities for provincial governments to innovate, given that labour standards for the vast majority of Canadian workers are set at the provincial level.

A sensitivity to social cohesion invites us to view the intensification of work schedules from a social, rather than an individual, standpoint. If one worker finds he is no longer able to participate in the chess club because he is subject to unpredictable overtime demands, that might be unfortunate for him and him alone. The chess club has one less member, and if its membership is now an odd number, one guy has to sit out every now and again. If this kind of intensification besets a large cross-section of workers, however, there will be a precipitous decline in the number of civic groups to which people belong. This is driven not only by the push to employ some people sixty hours a week, but also by the push to employ others only fifteen hours a week; if the latter workers have erratic schedules, the planning of leisure time becomes impossible. The necessity of being available at the drop of a hat for the few precious available hours of work precludes the making and keeping of other commitments. A consequence will be the privatization of leisure, as people unable to attend meetings of the now-defunct gardening club opt instead for the gardening channel on cable television, broadcasting twenty-four hours a day. People almost certainly will enjoy their leisure less; and at the same time the fellow feeling, exchange of information, and trust that can arise from civil society will also erode.

Schools and Neighbourhoods

The intensity of work schedules and the imperative that two or more household members work to make ends meet also creates problems for child care. There are, however, possible community-based solutions to these pressures that generate social cohesion.

UNICEF has pointed out the potential role of schools as sites of social-capital accumulation. This is true not only because of the socializing role of publicly-provided education reviewed in Chapter 4. Schools can contribute to social cohesion in more immediate ways. A neighbourhood school provides a location where children can stay after school while parents work. The social bonds forged on the playground are deepened with after-school activities; sports and cultural activities instill attitudes toward co-operation, teamwork, and tolerance. All the while, after-school child care relieves pressures on overworked parents. Moreover, contributing to the organization of after-school child care and activities provides opportunities for parents to build neighbourhood-based organizations, to interact with other parents, and thereby contribute to social cohesion.

These recommendations point in the opposite direction from current trends in school financing in Canada. In Halifax, indeed, the local school board has refused even to provide free *lunchtime* supervision of children, never mind after-school supervision. But other countries have successfully promoted this model of schools as foci of social cohesion. New South Wales in Australia, for example, provides a seamless schedule of before-school, lunchtime, and after-school activities for children.

Cultural Policy

The Canadian Senate defines social cohesion as "a community of shared values," perhaps a more broad concept than our working definition based on high returns to co-operative behaviour. Nevertheless, this official definition clearly shares some features of ours. Building social cohesion must involve coming to share beliefs and values. "People need to discuss their beliefs in order to come to share them," notes economist Shaun Hargreaves Heap matter-of-factly. How do these conversations come about? Hargreaves Heap's answer gives pride of place to the so-called cultural industries:

> Discussions ... take place informally in groups over lunch, in the pub, on the street and across the garden fence. This may not be obvious at first sight, but gossip about friends quite naturally involves comment on and evaluation of other people's behaviour and the same is often the case with the other central topic of discussion: what was seen the night before on TV or at the movies or in the sporting arena. It is in the discussion of behaviour in a 'soap' on TV or of a character in a film or a person on the sports field that people engage, albeit often implicitly, in a discussion of ideas.

The cultural industries (written media, film, broadcasting, music) of a nation provide the raw material for an ongoing discussion about values and beliefs. Similar arguments could be made for the other classes of cultural products. Conservation of heritage preserves the historical circumstances of a community as a backdrop for its contemporary activities; a museum that preserves for current visitors the conditions of habitant life, or that of the nineteenth-century Maritimes fisherman, provides a compelling picture of how one's forebears addressed their world. Our choices today about how to order our material life do not occur in a historical vacuum if we can refer to this well-conserved heritage. The (fine) arts may not reach as many people as the cultural industries or heritage sites, but represent the creative activity of a non-random minority charged with commenting on ways of seeing the world. Artists' output is especially influential with creators in the cultural industries and therefore has an important effect indirectly on large numbers of people. For all of these sectors, cultural products serve as the basis for discussions among members of society regarding values and beliefs.

Hargreaves Heap makes the further observation that "since the shared experience is a resource for such discussion, the character of shared beliefs that emerge from such discussion will depend on the material found in the shared experience. Of course, the outcome of discussions will depend on much else, but these seem simple inferences from the general idea that the output of any process depends on the inputs." A corollary of his insistence on content is this: domestic, or domestically-oriented, content will have a different impact than imported content. All Canadians can watch *Who Wants to Be a Millionaire?*; the shared experience could serve as the basis for the discussions that constitute national identity and social cohesion. But this is not enough; such discussions will be more relevant and more productive (in the specific ways we would like) to the extent that they are based on content more readily applicable to people's everyday reality. One good, though not perfect, predictor of whether the content will be germane to a people is if nationals of the country in question produce it. As long as consumers of cultural products continue to share political space as citizens of the same country, domestically-oriented content will be productive in these informal discussions in ways that imported content will not. These discussions underlined by Hargreaves Heap have important spillovers for other types of collective activity and "ways of living together" (UNESCO's simple definition of *culture*): most notably, for the process of democratic deliberation. Of course, to the extent that we are all citizens of the world, then openness to the world's cultural products is salutary. In Canada, this openness has never been denied.

Thus, domestic cultural products are, a priori, more likely than imported cultural products to generate positive spillovers when they serve as the basis for informal discussions about values and beliefs.

More specifically, such products will be better at generating national identity and social cohesion. In this way, domestic and imported cultural products are not perfectly interchangeable. They may be similar, but it is not clear that they are "like goods" as the language of international-trade negotiations would have it. Spanish economist Andreu Mas-Colell makes a distinction in this debate between protection of the production of national culture and protection of national cultural production: the appropriate goal of public policy is the former, but the only feasible way of achieving that goal is through the latter. Policy should seek to promote the production of national culture, in the sense that cultural products with domestically-oriented content will generate more useful social discussion; in practice, this veers dangerously close to regulating or controlling the thematic content of cultural production, which is antithetical to free expression. Protecting national cultural producers, while vulnerable to the usual attacks of free-trade proponents, may be the best feasible way of safeguarding national culture without dictating exactly what that culture is.

This is a novel rationale for Canada's cultural policy, which has never had the organic intellectual consistency of France's, for example, but which nevertheless, in fits and starts, has sought to preserve "shelf space" for the output of Canada's cultural industries. Seen through the prism of social cohesion, such initiatives are not merely, or even primarily, pork-barrel attempts to protect jobs in Canada. Instead, guaranteeing access to, and a reasonable supply of, Canadian cultural products promotes a necessary national conversation. Support for a "cultural exemption" from evolving international-trade regulations makes eminently good sense, even from a perspective friendly to free trade generally. Cultural products — novels, compact discs, films, dance productions — generate poorly-appreciated spinoffs in the form of social goods like cohesion.

Redistributive Public Finance

All of the foregoing recommendations — for child-centred defence of EI and equalization payments, for direct support of *groupes communautaires*, for labour standards and legislation — rely on a very active government at the federal, provincial, municipal, and even neighbourhood level. The oft-made assertion that social cohesion harnesses the energies of civil society in a way that can substitute for services provided in past decades by governments is only partly true. Indeed, civil society and social capital are complementary to government initiatives and policy making; that is, citizens' initiatives will tend to yield greater economic benefits when complemented by the appropriate government policies. Nevertheless, the kind of government involvement that is called for is different from both the classic post-war model exemplified by Lester Pearson and Pierre Elliott Trudeau and from the leaner "neo-conservative" model that came to the fore in the 1980s and 1990s. The public debate on taxation in Canada does not inspire optimism for a renewed call for progressive taxation. Yet public-opinion polls reveal that Canadians are not hostile to current levels of taxation per se; instead, they increasingly express dissatisfaction with the benefits that their taxes appear to provide.

An awareness of social cohesion and economic performance addresses taxpayers' concerns directly. Public-private partnerships to provide certain benefits of the welfare state can offer these services at a lower cost to taxpayers. Small infusions of public funds might have large effects on the well-being of many Canadians — the poor, the unemployed, the elderly. But such partnerships also generate spillovers in the connectedness of people in society — and this in turn promotes better economic performance, which could even generate higher tax revenues through a variety of indirect means. Moreover, the international evidence of inequality and economic growth presented in Chapter 5 demonstrates that, over time, a more equal income distribution and renewed social cohesion might strengthen support for fair and productive taxation, in a kind of virtuous circle.

In this connection, it is helpful to review a recent economic model elaborated by Columbia University's Xavier Sala-i-Martin while he was a visiting researcher at the International Monetary Fund. (That the following logic was developed within the corridors of the IMF gives us extraordinary occasion to be hopeful about the future.) Sala-i-Martin's model is inspired by the finding, discussed in Chapter 5, that transfer payments associated with social safety nets appear to increase, not depress, economic growth. He hypothesizes that transfers to the poor give them a greater stake in social peace; crime or other disruptive activities become relatively more costly for marginalized people if the relevant alternative is generous transfers. (Sala-i-Martin argues that in many cases wage subsidies will work better than just writing cheques to poor people: wage subsidies lower the cost to employers of hiring another worker.) The public welfare system, in this model, is a public good subject to congestion, just like interprovincial highways or the broadcast spectrum. Such public goods make private investments more productive and raise growth.

An interesting proposition of Sala-i-Martin's model is that the optimal way to finance the social safety net is via income taxes. This is more surprising than it may at first sound: the most efficient tax in most economic models is the hard-to-implement and infrequently-observed lump-sum tax. Like poll taxes, everyone just pays the same dollar amount, not a percentage of consumption or income. Lump-sum taxes do not distort incentives to work and invest the way that income taxes do. High-income people will work and invest less in the presence of high marginal tax rates; lump-sum taxes will not affect their decision to invest an extra dollar or work an hour more. Sala-i-Martin's result is closely tied to certain assumptions underlying his model, and should be taken with a grain of salt. It works as follows: Income taxes, by depressing investment in the usual way, do slow growth; but, Sala-i-Martin maintains, growth, if "excessive," also makes criminal activity more remunerative. The individual investor will not properly take into account this crime-enhancing aspect of her investment; however, higher income tax rates effectively dissuade her from investing "too much." Thus, the growth-impeding effects of income tax keep excessive growth in check and control the rising rate of crime that would accompany it, achieving an optimal and balanced result.

Perhaps the most compelling rationale for state action, but at the same time the least familiar to proponents of the welfare state, is the pervasive influence of multiple equilibria. Two apparently similar societies might evolve in very different directions because of tiny differences in their past. This happens because our propensity to co-operate with our neighbours and strangers is strongly influenced by our expectation that others will also co-operate. Generalized pessimism about the level of co-operative behaviour and generalized optimism are both possible outcomes. Government policy, through even relatively small support for community school boards or legislation of labour standards, can tip people's inclinations towards the good equilibrium. Policy becomes what economists call a "co-ordinating device." As all members of society respond to the new co-operative environment, the economy works more smoothly in the myriad ways detailed in the preceding chapters — and this can be achieved with comparatively small public investments.

Bibliographic Notes

Phipps (2001) demonstrates, among other things, the impact of moving on children, referenced in the text above. See also Phipps (1999) for a useful elaboration of a "child-centred" conception of economic well-being. Dayton-Johnson (2000a) is my study of rural/urban differences in social cohesion in Canada. Venne (1999) is a press account of political mobilization among *groupes communautaires* in Québec. Slaughter (1995) reviews the UAW action against GM in Flint, Michigan. Labour educator Alexandra Dagg (1997) provides a Canadian perspective on the intensification and casualization of work; see also Osberg's (1997) contribution to the same volume. For a discussion of shrinking free time in the USA, see Hunter (1999). The recent changes to the Ontario Employment Standards Act are reported in the 12 December 2000 *Toronto Star* (Canadian Press, 2000). Osberg (2001) documents international dispersion in average working hours per week: workers in the US are working, on average, nearly eight hours a week more than workers in some European countries. I consider the economics of cultural policy in Canada, and its relation to social cohesion, in Dayton-Johnson (2000b). Rabinovitch (1998) provides a useful overview of Canada's cultural policy over time; UNESCO (1996, p. 14) gives the four-word definition of culture used above. For overviews of the evolution of fiscal and social policy in Canada over the last two decades, see, respectively, Campbell (1999) and Prince (1999).

8

A New Vision of Social Cohesion

This final chapter will be a summing up of the ideas in the book so far, including enlightening (I hope) detours through the history of punk rock and feminist theory, and leading in the end to a call for a new vision of social cohesion in Canada and elsewhere.

A Review of the Terrain

This book has been inspired by two empirical observations, the first well-known to the point of banality, the other perhaps not so widely recognized. First, differences in levels of economic prosperity among countries in the world today are nothing short of astonishing. Second, the degree of knitted warmth that connects people varies widely from country to country. What is more interesting is that the two observations appear to be related: more knitted warmth not only makes people happy, it makes economies work better. This finding, which emerges from a host of economic studies, is a compelling motivation to better understand first, the link between prosperity and social cohesion, and second, the nature of social cohesion itself.

Probably the most startling evidence reviewed in Chapter 2 was the finding that countries where more people claimed to trust one another in 1980 had higher rates of economic growth in the subsequent twelve years. The researchers in this case controlled for the effect of educational attainment, the initial level of development, and the cost of investment goods in the economy. Other studies confirm and complement this fundamental result. Chapter 3 explores the microeconomic logic behind this result, sketching a series of simple economic models in which randomly-matched people interact in situations marked by strong incentives to behave opportunistically. Opportunism, however, turns out to be the least desirable outcome of the interaction: both people would prefer a co-operative outcome. This is the essence of the so-called "prisoners' dilemma." In a simple system where people are matched to play the prisoners' dilemma, the opportunity to invest in a publicly observable artifact called "social capital" makes co-operation more likely. In this context, "social cohesion" is modelled as a function of the sum of social-capital investments made by all the agents, with the proviso that social cohesion depreciates: investments made in the past weigh less heavily on agents today. Furthermore, the higher the level of social cohesion, the higher the rate of return on social capital today. Social cohesion becomes a sort of virtuous cycle. Of course, the failure to invest in social capital — to build personal and impersonal relationships, to join groups and form networks — becomes a sort of vicious cycle. Low social capital levels keep social cohesion low; low social cohesion dissuades people from co-operating. This is the nature of *multiple equilibria*: in a non-deterministic system, good things can happen, but so can bad ones.

The backdrop to this story is the assertion that the modern capitalist economy is as fundamentally a co-operative system as it is a competitive one. The much-heralded efficiency and prosperity delivered by the system relies, arguably, more on co-operation than it does on competition. This might strike a lot of readers as counterintuitive or fallacious, so let me repeat. Firms compete, it is true, in the market economy. When it works out, this keeps prices near the cost of production and prevents the extraction of surplus from consumers. What is remarkable is just how circumscribed this competition is, even in the idealized view of the most ardent proponents of the liberal economy. It is hemmed in by legal restrictions. There are laws against unfair competition based on "insider knowledge." There are laws against unfair practices to disadvantage your rivals. Most obviously, you cannot kill a dynamic manager at your rival's firm. Competition among firms and consumers is similarly, and perhaps even more significantly, constrained by social norms. Let's face it: there are mechanisms in place to discourage petty theft from supermarkets, but if more people wanted to steal things, they could probably get away with it. In the caricature of the competitive market economy propounded both by its most virulent opponents and its rather mealy-mouthed champions on the right, greed-crazed capitalist-minded consumers would be ripping off the supermarket all the time. Why don't they? A consciousness of co-operation is necessary to understand all the market exchanges that unfold over time, from the house painter who paints your house today and then bills you tomorrow, to the multi-million dollar loan extended to a large corporation, who must repay the loan over time.

Whether people honour agreements and contracts because they are afraid of prosecution or afraid of social ostracism, the effect is, in the first instance, the same. People more or less agree to follow the rules, formal and informal, of the system, without which the competitive market mechanism simply would not work. In just about every gesture undertaken by producers and consumers in the market economy there is an implicit or explicit act of co-operation. This would have been obvious to Adam Smith and many of the intellectual progenitors of the liberal view of the world. Some will object that crimes do occur, all the time, and they occur with greater frequency in some countries than they do in others. Contravention of formal and informal rules is not unknown. People do steal from stores, and in some places at certain times, theft is widespread; in the extreme, looting occurs. Some companies default on loans or on paying bondholders, and in some places, sometimes, corporate paper is generally worthless. These breakdowns of generalized co-operation only reinforce the point made in this book. When people co-operate, the system works better. No one would champion economic performance in Russia today or in an economy where food riots are occurring (as in Jamaica and Venezuela in the 1990s).

And this is where social cohesion makes a difference. In the vast interstices of the market-mediated society, for the millions of social interactions that the market does *not* mediate, social cohesion encourages co-operation; co-operation in turn makes the economy work better. This then, is the microeconomic logic that can explain the empirical correlation between measures of social cohesion like trust, and measures of economic performance, like growth rates.

The observed correlation between cohesion and economic performance is strengthened if one considers the relationship between social cohesion and broader measures of economic success, like the United Nations' Human Development Index. The HDI aggregates information on average income, educational attainment, and health, to gauge a nation's level of well-being. Chapter 4 demonstrated that disentangling cause and efffect in the relationship between education and social cohesion, still in its infancy as a research agenda, will likely be very difficult. Publicly-provided schooling gives students a shared experience and inculcates common values that construct a particularly strong form of social cohesion; more cohesive societies, meanwhile, are more likely to devote considerable resources to education. The chapter also reviewed a rich vein of health research demonstrating a connection between inequality and population health. More unequal societies, controlling for other characteristics, have worse health, as measured by things like mortality rates. One variety of explanation for that association is that unequal societies engender stress-inducing (and thus health-damaging) feelings of inferiority. Another suggests that inequality is bad for population health because those at the bottom of the income distribution have less access to those things that promote good health. This view is supported by recent research in Canada that finds no link between inequality in a city or province and its level of health; in Canada, universal health care effectively severs, or at least weakens, the link between one's income and one's access to health care.

This last result, relating inequality to population health, raises a more general question. Are all of the effects of social cohesion really effects of economic inequality? After all, a lot of the recent empirical research on international comparisons of growth rates emphasizes the negative impact of inequality, not social cohesion, on economic growth. Chapter 5 reviewed this research and concluded that economic equality and social cohesion are two different things. Economic inequality hampers growth largely by restricting the opportunities open to the poor; low or fraying social cohesion hampers growth by weakening the co-operative infrastructure of the market system. Indeed, much of the research on the negative role of inequality, with its emphasis on electoral and social conflict, really describes the effects of low social cohesion.

Unanswered Questions

The exploration of social cohesion and its links to the economy raises, arguably, more questions than it answers. Two, especially, loom large. First, is social cohesion a good or bad thing? Second, if it's a good thing, how can we have more of it about?

Having trumpeted the positive payoff of knitted warmth, Chapter 6 confronts the unpleasant claims about the "downside" of social cohesion. Groups can form to pursue joint objectives, but those objectives might be, well, objectionable. I proposed that the real question is: how well does social cohesion scale up? Groups through-out society might pursue their aims in a way that generates more trust generally, or alternatively, in ways that engender divisive conflict. The real controversy over social cohesion is mislaid. It is not a matter of whether social cohesion exists (it does), or whether it helps groups achieve collective goals (it does that too). Rather, the question is how high this knitted warmth scales up before the cohesive wholes begin to war among themselves. Two randomly-matched people from a neighbourhood might trust each other to undertake some kind of economic exchange; two randomly-matched people from different neighbourhoods might trust each other nearly as much (maybe up to a trust-requiring exchange worth a little less than the first one); two randomly-matched people from different cities might likewise trust each other; but two people drawn at random from two different provinces might not trust each other at all. That's the point where scaling up stops. Perhaps, as in many countries, that's the point at which two randomly-matched people are likely to be members of two different ethnic groups.

Another of the criticisms of social cohesion is that the term means different things to different people, or even to the same people. Once one begins to think about social cohesion, it seems to me that just about every story in the newspaper has to do with it. The sovereigntist movement in Québec? It's about social cohesion. The debate over health care? It's about social cohesion. NAFTA? Social cohesion. This universal relevance points out two things. First, the concept is incredibly useful and productive in trying to understand Canada today. Second, the concept is insufficiently refined. Some things really are *not* about social cohesion. Indeed, much of the enthusiasm for social cohesion on editorial pages today probably stems from imprecise usage of the term: an imprecise concept appears to encompass so much.

For this reason, it is especially useful to look at the concept in the cold, clinical light of social-science research. As we've used the term in this book, social cohesion is probably best measured by the likelihood that two total strangers will trust each other, even a little. That's all. And the most relevant scale by which to measure this cohesion is to insist that the two randomly-matched people are Canadian. (Or American, or Swiss, as long as they are from the same political jurisdiction.) This is because, to the extent that policy-makers can do anything to influence social cohesion, their action will be contained within national boundaries. Thus it makes sense to measure social cohesion on the basis of nationally-fielded surveys, for example. This national scale is moreover the appropriate one to judge whether social cohesion has successfully scaled up or not.

Nationalism

Even if a nation-state is privileged to have a high level of social cohesion (in the precise terms used in this book, meaning that *any* two nationals called upon to co-operate would do so) it is still subject to the "downside" critique. Nations, notoriously, can cohesively pursue insalubrious objectives. The history of the twentieth century is littered with examples of the excesses of nationalism. If the reader will indulge me, I'll consider a little illustration inspired by the halcyon days of punk rock music in the UK.

The Gang of Four was the name of one of the legion of post-punk bands that emerged in the UK in the grey and heady days of the early Thatcher years and in the immediate wake of the Sex Pistols. As their name suggests — invoking the then-current Maoist clique of the same name — they were quirkily political. More elegantly than any of the other bands of the time, the Leeds outfit managed to capture the central contradictions of the modern age. A greatest-hits collection, released well after the fact, was immodestly entitled *A Brief History of the Twentieth Century*. The cover art, by band member Jon King, succinctly provided just that: photographs of two coins side by side, two French francs. One is dated 1961, and is emblazoned with the classic lemma of 1798 — liberté, égalité, fraternité. The other, dated 1943, during the Nazi occupation, replaces that slogan with travail, famille, patrie. Liberty, equality, brotherhood; work, family, fatherland.

The juxtaposition is chilling, and evocative. On the one hand, the story has a happy ending; the ideology of the French Revolution, the font of modern liberal democracy and social order, reimposes itself over the fascist interlude. But in some sense, 1943 is still present in 1961: many — most — of those who brought about the pro-Nazi regime were still alive, and even those who opposed it bore its scars still. More generally, the Nazi interlude showed that it was possible to turn back the progression of democratic development. However, the 1943 slogan — travail, famille, patrie — served to unite France and the French during parlous times. Moreover, none of these concepts by itself, or even taken as a whole, is intrinsically fascist. But the 1943 franc reminds us that these concepts are susceptible to distortion by ideologies of national unity. Proponents of social cohesion in North America may argue that if social cohesion has favourable economic consequences, then any source of unity, any flag to rally round, is a valuable means to an end. It will strike some readers as a far-fetched comparison, but those proponents need to be constantly reminded of the extremes to which this argument can be stretched. For thousands of French Jews and socialists, the virtuous-sounding "work, family, fatherland" masked a murderous reality.

But it goes further. The problem with the 1943 rallying cry is not that it itself produced evil effects. The fascist focus on work, family life, and nationalism merely took advantage of pre-existing patterns of subjugation, patterns which endure still in workplaces, households, and national political economies — such as the late-1970s Britain in which the Gang of Four operated. This is the true message of the collage. King looked around at his co-workers, at the relationships between men and women, at the cynical manipulation of national symbols by national leaders, and bore witness that the fascist program itself lived on — beyond the deaths of its explicit proponents. Jorge Luis Borges, the late and great Argentine writer, expressed the problem with characteristic concision and force: "Mentally, Nazism is nothing but the exacerbation of a prejudice which afflicts all men: the certainty of the superiority of their fatherland, of their language, of their religion, of their blood."

These fears are not, I would argue, excessive. Few things generate fellow feeling as effectively as an obsessive hatred for outsiders, suitably defined. In light of the well-known pathologies of nationalism and the downside of social cohesion, let me rephrase the two big questions mentioned earlier. (1) How can we make people feel more interconnected? And (2) how can we accomplish number (1) in a way that respects differences? In many ways, it is the intolerance toward differences that makes tight-knit communities repugnant to so many observers within and without. Nationalism promulgated *à outrance* is defined by intolerance: this becomes a problem because nationals will inevitably encounter people who are different, either on the battlefield, or within their own society, or both.

The Welfare State

Chapter 7 attempts, partially at least, to address the conditions under which social cohesion will scale up successfully, in the context of what policy-makers can actually do. (And since, at least at some remove, we choose our policy-makers, this is what *we* can do about things.) Moreover, at least in the hope of fostering further debate, I will suggest that these recommendations sidestep the overzealous nationalist recipe for generating knitted warmth among a country's residents. Taken as a whole, the recommendations made in Chapter

7 can be easily recast as a call for a renewal of the welfare state in Canada: renewed commitment to equalization payments, generous unemployment insurance and other forms of social assistance, public investment in depressed regions, and progressive taxation. Each of those policies (and others, like public action in the realm of cultural production) is logically supported in terms of generating social cohesion. Each of those policies (and others, like public action in the realm of cultural production) is logically supported in terms of generating social cohesion; however, the very idea of the welfare state can generate social cohesion.

This is perhaps most clear in the analogy made by economist Xavier Sala-i-Martin (reviewed in Chapter 7) between the social-assistance system and publicly-funded physical infrastructure. Social-assistance, paid for by all taxpayers in this model makes anti-social behaviour less attractive to the poor. Taking this one step further, the social-assistance regime encourages all members of society — those paying in and those receiving benefits in times of hard luck — to see themselves as part of the same network of co-operative behaviour that makes the market economy work better. As the system is universal in scope, no one contemplates opting out. This common consciousness of being part of a single polity can generate social cohesion at a national level in precisely the way the concept has been defined in this book.

Look at the analogy from a local level. Municipal governments in Canada build and maintain sports facilities, playing fields, swimming pools. This is the infrastructure in which social cohesion can develop. Citizens in these municipalities form, at all levels of organizational sophistication, associations, like softball teams and softball leagues. A well-patronized park is a place where parents can be reasonably assured that other children will be playing, thus providing a social meeting ground for kids; more formally, children's groups can be formed by parents or the municipality or both. The interlocking, mutually-reinforcing roles of publicly-provided infrastructure and civil society are quite clear. Furthermore, publicly-provided infrastructure provides fellow feeling in a way that private initiatives can do only with difficulty. No one is prevented from using the park whereas private sports facilities require you to present your membership card. Both types of facilities can be expected to generate social cohesion, but only the public facilities are founded on the notion of inclusion of all.

The World as a Problem of Insufficient Insurance

It may surprise some readers (including some economists who disagree with the statement), but a significant fraction of theoretical and empirical work in economics in the last quarter century has been concerned with *insurance*, broadly construed. This might sound strange largely because insurance is seen as the domain of pushy salesmen to protect us against the loss of our houses to fires. Weighty stuff, but several orders of magnitude less important than, say, poverty. But insurance, and the insecurity it seeks to ameliorate, are far more important than this limited conception.

This is especially true in development economics, the economic study of low-income countries. Poverty is the fundamental problem, but this is an overly unidimensional way of looking at the problems of well-being. Most people in poor countries are, arguably, afflicted with insecurity to a greater degree than they are beset by absolute poverty. And many of the one-billion-plus absolutely poor would be better off with some insurance. This is not a trite recommendation that fire and theft insurance are the answer to the third world's woes. More fundamentally, poor people in the developing world are faced with wild and unpredictable variations in their command over resources from year to year. Vagaries of climate, war, and international price movements can mean the difference between life and death. The ability to smooth their livelihoods over good and bad times — which is all that insurance is, after all — would make life a lot easier even if their average income level were to remain unchanged.

What is remarkable is the degree to which people in poor agrarian economies and destitute urban neighbourhoods in poor countries band together to insure one another. How is this accomplished under such unpromising conditions? The same way that private insurance companies work in Canada: they take money from people having a good year, and pay out money to those having a bad year. Thus village economies in Asia, Africa, and Latin America exhibit creative schemes whereby those with good crop yields transfer resources to those less fortunate this year. Next year, today's recipients of assistance might be helping out those who are paying out today. In urban Latin America, collective soup kitchens pool resources from all the households in a neighbourhood to ensure that no one starves as a result of temporary (or long-term) destitution.

Economic insecurity is relevant in Canada as well. The risk of unemployment and underemployment, the risk of insufficient resources in one's old age, the risk of becoming a single parent, the risk of illness and disability, are potentially catastrophic outcomes that quite justifiably concern Canadians. And still another prism for understanding the welfare state is that it is a giant, socially shared insurance mechanism. High income-earners pay in; those who succumb to one of the risks mentioned above receive assistance. Tomorrow the roles of net recipients or net contributors might be reversed. The variations in our well-being and livelihood that would obtain in an uninsured world are significantly dampened. This makes us more willing to take certain chances — on acquiring an education, on moving to take a new job, on investing in a potentially productive new idea.

It may also make us feel a deeper sense of belonging. The difference between the ingenious insurance arrangements of Third World villages and the social insurance of the Canadian welfare state is instructive. In the former case, poor people draw upon social, cohesion to provide insurance to each other. Without social cohesion, such informal schemes would not work: I would take the payout this year if my crop output were low, but when it came time for me to pay in, I would refuse or leave the village. If there were social pressures like ostracism within the village to enforce this arrangement, the fortunate this year would be dissuaded from opting out. Social cohesion makes insurance possible. In the case of the welfare state, I am suggesting that the causation might run in the opposite direction: insurance generates social cohesion. Of course, the welfare state would be impossible in the absence of some shared vision of its importance among voters and lawmakers. But I propose that the existence and maintenance of the welfare state will in turn bind participants in the scheme together.

Many commentators in Canada will view this policy conclusion with a jaundiced eye. For them, the welfare state is discredited, and a leaner and meaner style of governance is appropriate. To them I hasten to point out two things. First, the empirical evidence is on my side. Generous social-welfare systems are associated with higher growth. The correlation is not ironclad: governments can dispense money to poor people by means of ill-designed programs to no discernible effect. But well-designed and administered social-welfare programs correct problems of the market economy. But more important, this book arrives at its conclusion by means other than what critics would regard as the same old tired lefty logic: the argument here is that the policies associated with the welfare state are just about the best thing that governments can do to foster social cohesion. Moreover, social cohesion depends on a vital civil society of formal and informal associations. In this view, the state can provide the infrastructure (like parks and social insurance), but networks and trust form in largely private interactions among people. The state can make those kind of positive interactions more likely, or more productive, or more remunerative, but it cannot make them happen. This public-private aspect of social cohesion transcends many of the traditional left-right political dichotomies.

Finally, I want to point out that the policies outlined in Chapter 7 would not necessarily be right for other countries. In fact in developing countries, I would recommend even more enthusiastically that government occupy the commanding heights of the economy. Nevertheless, the concrete problems facing poor countries are sufficiently different, and the resources available sufficiently lower, that a mechanical translation of the welfare-state recommendations of Chapter 7 to Ukraine or Vietnam would be irresponsible. Similarly, the social cleavages besetting other countries — for example, the artificial postcolonial countries of much of sub-Saharan Africa — are so much deeper than those afflicting Canada that measures considered here for Canada are almost guaranteed to be insufficient there.

The New Community

So we have seen that we as citizens can encourage an activist state to implement policies that will promote fellow feeling and interconnectedness. The second challenge mentioned above is how to prevent intolerance along the way, how to respect differences. Although this issue certainly lies within the purview of policy-makers, it is well outside the realm of *economic* policy and, as such, beyond the scope of this book. It's worth emphasizing that this book is supposed to explain what social cohesion is and to show that it has an economic payoff. It's not a treatise on what social cohesion should be. But I will outline a framework elaborated by feminist theorist Iris Marion Young (a professor or political science at the University of Chicago) that I have found quite fruitful in thinking about this issue.

Feminism in the last quarter century has grappled with the possibly contradictory aims of acting collectively for certain political ends while at the same time respecting differences. Advancing the cause of equal rights for women has required unity, based ostensibly on a uniform set of "women's needs" or "women's characteristics." This tendency toward seeing similarity among women has abruptly come up against demands to respect diversity — diversity among women of colour, lesbians and straight women, women of different generations, women in the first and third worlds. It is not surprising then, that there should be within feminist thought some creative proposals to solve our dilemma regarding a cohesive but not exclusive social ideal.

What is refreshing about Young's proposition is that she pits our ideas of the cohesive small-town community, a powerful image in the social cohesion debate as well, against the bright lights of the big city. The discussion is revealing. Critics of the downside of social cohesion have acknowledged the benefits of membership in a tight-knit small-town community — you can buy goods at the corner store on credit — but wonder if these benefits are not swamped by the asphyxiating push toward conformity. People frozen out of their small towns have long looked toward the modern metropolis. As Young writes, "For many people deemed deviant in the closeness of the face-to-face community in which they lived, whether 'independent' women or socialists or gay men and lesbians, the city has offered a welcome anonymity and some measure of freedom." Consider the city, rather than the small town, as a model for social cohesion. After all, the fundamental problem for instilling social cohesion is how to widen the radius of trust beyond the kin network to include, essentially, strangers. This is a move from the trust found in small towns toward a big-city style of trust. As Young writes, "City life is the 'being-together' of strangers."

Young goes on to explore why it is that people find the big city so attractive, even when they are wedded to the ideal of community: "Even many of the most staunch proponents of decentralized community love to show visiting friends around the Boston or San Francisco or New York in which they live, climbing up towers to see the glitter of lights and sampling the fare at the best ethnic restaurants." She concludes that cities are exciting because the experience of urban life embodies essentially limitless possibilities, endless combinations of neighbourhoods, hours of the day, types of encounters. Commitment to this unknowable and ungraspable whole is a commitment, simultaneously, to diversity and at the same time to being together: "Strangers encounter one another, either face to face or through media, often remaining strangers and yet acknowledging their contiguity in living and the contributions each makes to the other."

Of course, the city, just as the small town, has its downside. Many people in cities are quite intolerant of differences. Contiguity together with anonymity provides better opportunity for crime. Congestion in every sense eats up resources as well as providing togetherness. Just as enthusiasts of the small town have made a decision to model ideal human relations on the good aspects of communities, so an urban model of being together focuses on the ideal aspects of the model, always cognizant of the downside. Thus Young sketches an ideal of the "unoppressive city," which she defines as "openness to unassimilated otherness." Unassimilated, because there is no attempt to override differences.

The means of constructing social cohesion might not really be different in the city than they are in our old small-town ideal: you join groups ranging from highly formalized organizations to spontaneous gatherings. And the contribution of such associational activity to forming social networks in the urban model is arguably higher than in the rural one. After all, joining one more group in the city connects a person to at least a few people she doesn't know right now; joining one more group in the small town might merely put one into contact with the same old folks. This aspect of small-town life is lampooned by Stephen Leacock in *Sunshine Sketches of a Little Town* (1912):

> ... [Y]ou will easily understand that of course everybody belongs to the Knights of Pythias and the Masons and the Oddfellows, just as they all belong to the Snow Shoe Club and the Girls' Friendly Society ... In Mariposa practically everybody belongs to the Knights of Pythias just as they do to everything else. That's the great thing about the town and that's what makes it so different from the city. Everybody is in everything.

It may be easier to join more groups in a small town like Mariposa, but it's also less meaningful.

This model of being together holds great promise for building social cohesion in a new and purposive way. This sounds distinctively compatible with the laudable conception of Canada as a multicultural mosaic. It is also an ideal that Canada is pretty far from achieving. It is one thing to espouse respect for other world views and another to force others to abide by the Anglo-American liberal political philosophy enshrined in the Constitution. Not assimilating otherness might sometimes require recognition of communal rights not entirely compatible with individual rights elsewhere. The current furore over the Delgamuukw decision and the Nisga'a treaty show that this is a messy business. The successful establishment of Nunavut demonstrates likewise a considerable will to move in this direction in the relationship between Canada and its First Nations. The continuing acrimony over the precise nature of the collective identity of Québec (notwithstanding the "fatigue" that all sides to the debate are said to feel regarding the issue) is another gaping bit of unfinished business in the matter of assimilating otherness.

Parting Words

The simple message of this book is that knitted warmth among people has an economic payoff. The possibility that currently fashionable liberal economic policies might fray the social fabric is sometimes portrayed as a regrettable necessity, one that will be compensated by increased growth and prosperity. The research reviewed in this book shows that things are more complicated than that. Social cohesion has in no small measure been instrumental in creating prosperity in today's economies. Liberalization ignorant of this fact risks throwing out the baby with the bathwater. Consequently, the important work of promoting prosperity must include invigorating communities and social networks just as assiduously as invigorating investment in plants and equipment and in education and training.

Not a few readers, nevertheless, will argue that knitted warmth should be sought for its own sake. Humans form groups; that's what they do. Such readers might find it offensive that people need to be told there is an instrumental economic by-product from group formation. The intrinsic value of social cohesion could be the subject of another book (or better yet, a novel or play or poem). That's not what I've set out to do here. John Ralston Saul (1999, p. 460) recently deplored the "received wisdom in the economic-administrative manner," the economist's way of viewing the world, "delivered with the assurance of religious texts." In an environment dominated by this type of discourse, it may be that the only way to demonstrate the value of social cohesion is to demonstrate its economic value. I don't know if this is an accurate understanding of current reality, and, as an economist, I may be insufficiently objective to say. But critics of globalization, which is above all an extensive and intensive encroachment of markets and market logic, can in any case take solace in the fact that pretty conventional economic reasoning leads to a championing of civil society, voluntary groups, trust, and public action. I'll limit myself to insisting that economic prosperity and rich social interconnectedness are valid goals to be pursued in Canada today. If I have shown that they are happily compatible, then so much the better.

Bibliographic Notes

Check out the Gang of Four's greatest hits (Gang of Four, 1990); to situate the Gang of Four and punk rock in the larger narrative of cultural history, consult Marcus (1989). The links from Marcus's book to the subject matter of the book you're reading might surprise you. Borges made his comment on the fascism latent in all nationalism before the PEN Club of Argentina when Hitler was still alive, and against the backdrop of the Perón dictatorship in his own country. He is quoted in Vargas Llosa (1999). Young (1990) is the essay from which I draw extensively toward the close of this chapter; see her more recent book (Young, 2000) for a fuller elaboration of the themes in the essay.

Bibliography

Aghion, Philippe, Eve Caroli, and Cecilia Garcia-Peñolosa. (2000). Inequality and economic growth: The perspective of the new growth theories. *Journal of Economic Literature, 37*, 1615–60.

Alesina, Alberto, and Allen Drazen. (1991). Why are stabilizations delayed? *American Economic Review, 81*, 1170–88.

Alesina, Alberto, and Roberto Perotti. (1996). Income distribution, political instability, and investment. *European Economic Review, 40*, 1203–1228.

Alesina, Alberto, and Dani Rodrik. (1994). Distributive politics and economic growth. *Quarterly Journal of Economics, 109*, 465–490.

Baland, J.-M., and J.-P. Platteau. (1995). Does heterogeneity hinder collective action? *Cahiers de la Faculté des sciences économiques et sociales de Namur, Serie Recherche No. 146, Collection "Développement."*

Barro, Robert J. (1991). Economic growth in a cross section of countries. *The Quarterly Journal of Economics, 106*, 407–444.

Bénabou, Roland. (1996). Inequality and growth. *NBER Macroeconomics Annual, 11*, 11–74.

Bénabou, Roland. (2000). Unequal societies: Income distribution and the social contract. *American Economic Review, 90*, 96–129.

Bernard, Paul. (1999). La cohésion sociale: Critique dialectique d'un quasi-concept. *Lien social et politiques, 41*, 47–59.

Bourdieu, Pierre. (1986). The forms of capital. In J. Richardson, ed., *Handbook of theory and research for the sociology of education.* Westport, CT: Greenwood Press.

Bowles, Samuel, and Herbert Gintis. (2000). Walrasian economics in retrospect. *The Quarterly Journal of Economics, 15*, 1411–40.

Brooks, Patricia. (2000, March 26). Man finds $1,000 bag of toonies, returns it. *Chronicle-Herald* (Halifax), p. A1.

Buckler, Ernest. (1952). *The mountain and the valley.* Toronto. New Canadian Library, McClelland & Stewart Ltd.

Campbell, Robert M. (1999). The fourth fiscal era: Can there be a 'post-neo-conservative' fiscal policy? In Leslie A. Pal, ed., *How Ottawa Spends 1999–2000*, Don Mills, ON: Oxford University Press.

Canadian Press (2000, 12 December). 60-hr work week law nears approval, *Toronto Star.*

Coleman, James. (1990). *Foundations of social theory.* Cambridge, MA: Harvard University Press.

Crane, David. (2000, March 25). Economists finally discover social capital. *Toronto Star.*

Dagg, Alexandra. (1997). Worker representation and protection in the "new economy." In *Collective reflection on the changing workplace, Report of the Advisory Committee on the Changing Workplace.* Ottawa: Department of Labour.

Dayton-Johnson, Jeff. (1999). Irrigation organization in Mexican unidades de riego. *Irrigation and Drainage Systems, 13*, 55–74.

Dayton-Johnson, Jeff. (2000a). *Social cohesion and the rural economy in Canada*, mimeo, Dalhousie University.

Dayton-Johnson, Jeff. (2000b). What's different about cultural products? Report prepared for Department of Canadian Heritage. Hull QC: Department of Canadian Heritage.

Dayton-Johnson, Jeff. (2001). *Social capital, social cohesion, community: A microeconomic perspective*, mimeo, Dalhousie University.

de Tocqueville, Alexis. (1835/1840). *Democracy in America.* Specially edited and abridged for the modern reader by Richard D. Heffner. New York: New American Library, 1956.

DiManno, Rosie. (2000, January 21). A small price to pay for the country's soul on ice. *Toronto Star.*

Durlauf, Steven N. (1999). The case "against" social capital. *Focus, University of Wisconsin - Madison Institute for Research on Poverty, 20*(3) pp. 1–5.

Faulkner, William. (1948). *Intruder in the dust.* New York: Random House.

Feldman, Tine Rossing, and Susan Assaf. (1999). Social capital: Conceptual frameworks and empirical evidence. *Social Capital Initiative Working Paper No. 5*, The World Bank.

Fife, Robert (2000, February 23). HRDC employee says he was warned Ottawa would not 'tolerate dissent' over grants. *National Post.*

Foster, Peter. (2000, October 27). Of boiling frogs and globaloney. *National Post.*

Fukuyama, Francis. (1995). *Trust: The social virtues and the creation of prosperity.* New York: The Free Press.

Fukuyama, Francis. (1999). *The great disruption: Human nature and the reconstitution of social order.* New York: The Free Press.

Gang of Four. (1990). *A brief history of the twentieth century.* Warner Bros. Records 26448-2.

Gradstein, Mark, and Moshe Justman. (2000). Human capital, social capital, and public schooling. *European Economic Review, 44,* 879–890.

Granovetter, Mark. (1985). Economic action and social structure: The problem of embeddedness. *American Journal of Sociology, 91,* 481–510.

Hargreaves Heap, Shaun. (1999). Social capital and the economy. In Mark Setterfield, ed., *Growth, employment and inflation: Essays in honour of John Cornwall.* New York: St. Martins Press.

Helliwell, John F. (1996a). Do borders matter for social capital? Economic growth and civic culture in U.S. states and Canadian provinces. *Working Paper No. 5863.* Cambridge, MA: National Bureau of Economic Research.

Helliwell, John F. (1996b). Economic growth and social capital in Asia, *Working Paper No. 5470.* Cambridge, MA: National Bureau of Economic Research.

Helliwell, John F. (1998). *How much do national borders matter?* Washington, DC: The Brookings Institution.

Helliwell, John F. (2000). Globalization: Myths, facts, and consequences. C.D. Howe Institute Benefactors Lecture. Available: http://www.cdhowe.org/PDF/helliwell.pdf.

Hunter, Mark. (1999, November). Les salariés américains aimeraient le temps de vivre. *Le Monde diplomatique,* 18–19.

Kandori, Michinori. (1992). Social norms and community enforcement. *Review of Economic Studies, 59,* 63–80.

Kawachi, Ichiro, and Bruce P. Kennedy. (1999). Income inequality and health: Pathways and mechanisms. *HSR: Health Services Research, 34,* 215–227.

Kawachi, Ichiro, Bruce P. Kennedy, K. Lochner, and D. Prothrow-Stith. (1997). Social capital, income inequality, and mortality. *American Journal of Public Health, 87,* 1491–1498.

Kennedy, B.P., I. Kawachi, R. Glass, and D. Prothrow-Stith. (1998). Income distribution, socioeconomic status, and self-rated health: A U.S. multi-level analysis. *British Medical Journal, 317,* 917–921.

Knack, Stephen. (1999). Social capital, growth and poverty: A survey of cross-country evidence. *Social Capital Initiative Working Paper No. 7.* The World Bank.

Knack, Stephen. (2000). Trust, associational life and economic performance in the OECD. Paper prepared for the HRDC-OECD International Symposium on the Contribution of Investment in Human and Social Capital to Sustained Economic Growth and Well-Being, Québec City.

Knack, Stephen, and Philip Keefer. (1997). Does social capital have an economic payoff? A cross-country investigation. *The Quarterly Journal of Economics, 112,* 1251–1288.

La Porta, Rafael, Florencio López-de-Silanés, Andrei Shleifer, and Robert W. Vishny. (1997). Trust in large organizations. *American Economic Review (Papers and Proceedings), 87,* 333–338.

Lavis, John N., and Gregory L. Stoddart. (2000). *Social cohesion and health,* mimeo, McMaster University.

Leacock, Stephen. (1912). *Sunshine sketches of a little town.* Toronto: New Canadian Library, McClelland & Stewart Ltd.

Luce, R. Duncan, and Howard Raiffa. (1957). *Games and decisions: Introduction and critical survey.* New York: John Wiley & Sons. [1989 republication by Dover Publications, Inc., New York].

Lynch, John W., George Davey Smith, George A. Kaplan, and James S. House. (2000). Income inequality and mortality: Importance to health of individual income, psychosocial environment, or material conditions. *British Medical Journal, 320,* 1200–1204.

MacLean, Brian K. (2000). Canada's Economy in the Newspapers, various editions. Available: http://www.geocities.com/Wall-Street/8691/index.html.

Marcus, Greil. (1989). *Lipstick traces: A secret history of the twentieth century.* Cambridge, MA: Harvard University Press.

Mas-Colell, Andreu. (1999). Should cultural goods be treated differently? *Journal of Cultural Economics, 23,* 87–93.

McCallum, John. (1995). National borders matter: Canada-U.S. regional trade patterns. *American Economic Review, 85,* 615–623.

Milanovic, Branko. (1998). *Income, inequality, and poverty during the transition from planned to market economy.* Washington, DC: The World Bank.

Mousnier, Roland. (1974/1980). *Les institutions de la France sous la monarchie absolue, 1598-1789. Tome I, Société et État; Tome II, Les organes de l'État et la société.* Paris: Presses Universitaires de France.

Muntaner, C., and J. Lynch. (1999). Income inequality, social cohesion and class relations: A critique of Wilkinson's neo-Durkheimian research program. *International Journal of Health Services, 29*, 59–81.

Narayan, Deepa, and Lant Pritchett. (1999). Cents and sociability: Household income and social income in rural Tanzania. *Economic Development and Cultural Change, 47*, 873–97.

North, Douglass C. (1990). *Institutions, institutional change and economic performance.* New York: Cambridge University Press.

Okuno-Fujiwara, Masahiro, and Andrew Postlewaite. (1995). Social norms in random matching games. *Games and Economic Behavior, 9*, 79–109.

Olson, Mancur. (1965). *The logic of collective action.* Cambridge, MA: Harvard University Press.

Osberg, Lars. (1997). A personal reflection on the collective reflection. In *Collective reflection on the changing workplace, Report of the Advisory Committee on the Changing Workplace.* Ottawa: Department of Labour.

Osberg, Lars. (2000). *Long run trends in economic inequality in five countries: A birth cohort view.* mimeo. Halifax, NS: Dalhousie University.

Osberg, Lars. (2001). *Nobody to play with.* mimeo. Halifax, NS: Dalhousie University.

Osberg, Lars, and Andrew Sharpe. (2000). Comparison of trends in GDP and economic well-being: The Impact of Social Capital, paper presented at the Symposium on the Contribution of Human and Social Capital to Sustained Economic Growth and Well-Being in Canada, HRDC and OECD, Québec City.

Ostrom, Elinor. (1990). *Governing the commons: The evolution of institutions for collective action.* New York: Cambridge University Press.

Perotti, Roberto. (1994). Income distribution and investment. *European Economic Review, 38*, 827–835.

Persson, Torsten, and Guido Tabellini. (1994). Is inequality harmful for growth? *American Economic Review, 84*, 600–621.

Phipps, Shelley. (1999). Economics and the well-being of Canadian children, (The Innis Lecture). *Canadian Journal of Economics, 32*, 1135–1163.

Phipps, Shelley. (2001). *Social cohesion and the well-being of Canadian children,* mimeo, Dalhousie University.

Polanyi, Karl. (1944). *The great transformation*. New York: Rinehart & Company.

Portes, Alejandro. (1998). Social capital: Its origins and applications in modern sociology. *Annual Review of Sociology, 24*, 1–24.

Portes, Alejandro, and Patricia Landolt. (1996). The downside of social capital. *The American Prospect, 26*, 18–21.

Portes, Alejandro, and Patricia Landolt. (2000). Social capital: Promise and pitfalls of its role in development. *Journal of Latin American Studies, 32*, 529–547.

Prescott, Edward C. (1998). Needed: A theory of total factor productivity (Lawrence R. Klein Lecture 1997). *International Economic Review, 39*, 525–551.

PRI. (1999). *Sustaining growth, human development and social cohesion in a global world*. Ottawa: Policy Research Initiative.

Prince, Michael J. (1999). From health and welfare to stealth and farewell: Federal social policy, 1980-2000. In Leslie A. Pal, ed., *How Ottawa spends 1999–2000*. Don Mills, ON: Oxford University Press Canada.

Putnam, Robert D., and Thad Williamson. (2000, November 2). Pourquoi les Américains ne sont pas heureux. *Le Monde*.

Putnam, Robert D., with Robert Leonardi and Raffaella Y. Nanetti. (1993). *Making democracy work: Civic traditions in modern Italy*. Princeton, NJ: Princeton University Press.

Rabinovitch, Victor. (1998). The social and economic rationales for Canada's domestic cultural policies. In Dennis Browne, ed., *The culture/trade quandary: Canada's policy options*. Ottawa: Centre for Trade Policy and Law, Carleton University, 25–47.

Raphael, Dennis. (2000). Health inequalities in Canada: Current discourses and implications for public health action. *Critical Public Health, 10*, 193–216.

Ray, Debraj. (1998). *Development economics*. Princeton, NJ: Princeton University Press.

Rodrik, Dani. (1996). Understanding economic policy reform. *Journal of Economic Literature, 34*, 9–41.

Rodrik, Dani. (1998). Where did all the growth go? External shocks, social conflict, and growth collapses. *Working Paper No. 6350*. Cambridge, MA: National Bureau of Economic Research.

Rose, Carol M. (2001). Common property, regulatory property, and environmental protection: Comparing common pool resources to tradable environmental allowances. In Thomas Dietz, Nives Dolšak, Elinor Ostrom, Paul Stern, Susan Stonich, Elke Weber, eds., *Institutions for Managing the Commons*. Washington, DC: National Academy Press.

Rosell, Stephen A. (1999). *Renewing governance: Government in the information age*. Don Mills, ON: Oxford University Press Canada.

Ross, Nancy A., Michael C. Wolfson, James R. Dunn, Jean-Marie Berthelot, George A. Kaplan, and John W. Lynch. (2000). Relation between income inequality and mortality in Canada and in the United States: Cross sectional assessment using census data and vital statistics. *British Medical Journal, 320*, 898–902.

Sala-i-Martin, Xavier. (1997). Transfers, social safety nets, and economic growth. *IMF Staff Papers, 44*, 81–102.

Salutin, Rick. (2000 January 20). In defence of subsidies for millionaires. *The Globe and Mail*, p. A18.

Saul, John Ralston. (1999). *Reflections of a Siamese twin*. Toronto: Penguin Books Canada.

Seabright, Paul. (1997). Transferability of collective property rights: Does trade destroy trust? In John Roemer, ed., *Property rights, incentives and welfare*. London: IAE/Macmillan, 94–111.

Sharpe, Andrew. (2000). The stylized facts of the Canada-U.S. manufacturing productivity gap. Paper presented at the Centre for the Study of Living Standards Conference on the Canada-U.S. Manufacturing Productivity Gap, Ottawa, Ontario, January 21-22, 2000.

Slaughter, Jane. (1995 April). Addicted to overtime. *The Progressive, 59*.

Smith, Adam. (1759). *A theory of moral sentiments*.

Smith, Adam. (1776). *The wealth of nations*. Edited, with an introduction and notes by Edward Canaan, New York: The Modern Library.

Srinivasan, T.N. (1994). Human development: A new paradigm or reinvention of the wheel? *American Economic Review, Papers and Proceedings, 84*. 238–243

SSCSAST. (1999). Final report on social cohesion, Standing Senate Committee on Social Affairs, Science and Technology, Canadian Parliament, Ottawa.

Temple, Jonathan. (2000). Growth effects of education and social capital in the OECD, unpublished manuscript, Nuffield College, Oxford University.

Temple, Jonathan, and Paul A. Johnson. (1998). Social capability and economic growth. *The Quarterly Journal of Economics, 113*, 965–990.

Townson, Monica. (1999). *Health and wealth: How social and economic factors affect our well being.* Toronto: Canadian Centre for Policy Alternatives/James Lorimer & Co.

UNDP [United Nations Development Programme]. (1999). *Human development report.* New York: Oxford University Press.

UNESCO. (1996). *Our creative diversity, Report of the World Commission on Culture and Development.* Paris: United Nations Educational, Scientific and Cultural Organization.

Vargas Llosa, Mario. (1999). Borges, político, *Letras Libres* (Mexico City), November, pp. 24–26.

Venne, Michel. (1999, November 2). Groupes communautaires: entre l'État et l'individu. *Le Devoir*, Éditorial.

Walker, Alice. (1988). *The third life of grange copeland.* (originally published 1970). New York: Pocket Books.

Williamson, Oliver E., Michael L. Wachter, and Jeffrey E. Harris. (1975). Understanding the employment relation: The analysis of idiosyncratic exchange. *Bell Journal of Economics, 6*, 250–280.

Woolley, Francis. (2001). *Social cohesion and voluntary activity: Making connections*, mimeo, Carleton University.

World Bank. (1999). *World development report 1999/2000.* New York: Oxford University Press for the International Bank for Reconstruction and Development.

World Bank. (2000). *World development indicators.* Washington, DC: The International Bank for Reconstruction and Development.

World Values Study Group. (1999). World Values Survey 1981–1984 and 1990–1993 [Computer file]. 2nd ICPSR version. Ann Arbor, MI: Institute for Social Research [producer]; Ann Arbor, MI: Inter-university Consortium for Political and Social Research [distributor].

Wynn, G. (1987). On the margins of empire (1760–1840). In C. Brown, ed., *The illustrated history of Canada.* Toronto, ON: Key Porter Books.

Young, Irene Marion. (1990). The ideal of community and the politics of difference. In Linda J. Nicholson, ed., *Feminism/Postmodernism.* New York and London: Routledge.

Young, Irene Marion. (2000). *Inclusion and democracy.* New York: Oxford University Press.

Index